MALCOLM X

Other titles in the
People Who Made History series:

PEOPLE WHO MADE HISTORY

MALCOLM X

Jason Hunter, *Book Editor*

Daniel Leone, *President*
Bonnie Szumski, *Publisher*
Scott Barbour, *Managing Editor*
David M. Haugen, *Series Editor*

GREENHAVEN
PRESS®

THOMSON

GALE

San Diego • Detroit • New York • San Francisco • Cleveland
New Haven, Conn. • Waterville, Maine • London • Munich

For more information, contact
Greenhaven Press
27500 Drake Rd.
Farmington Hills, MI 48331-3535
Or you can visit our Internet site at http://www.gale.com

LIBRARY OF CONGRESS CATALOGING-IN-PUBLICATION DATA

Malcolm X / Jason Hunter, book editor.
    p. cm. — (People who made history)
Includes bibliographical references and index.
ISBN 0-7377-1492-1 (pbk. : alk. paper) — ISBN 0-7377-1491-3 (lib. : alk. paper)
    1. X, Malcolm, 1925–1965. 2. African American Muslims—Biography. I. Hunter, Jason. II. Series.
BP223.Z8 L57627 2004
320.54'092—dc21   2002035336

Printed in the United States of America

CONTENTS

became intensely attracted to the preachings of Elijah Muhammad's Nation of Islam. Malcolm, however, wanted more than to be just another Nation member. He had his own beliefs to espouse.

Chapter 3: The Nation of Islam

Chapter 4: Assassination

Muslim Mosque, Inc., would soon bring him under even closer scrutiny. This time, it was not just the FBI that was watching; the Nation of Islam had become his enemy as well.

Chapter 5: Malcolm's Legacy

FOREWORD

In the vast and colorful pageant of human history, a handful of individuals stand out. They are the men and women who have come variously to be called "great," "leading," "brilliant," "pivotal," or "infamous" because they and their deeds forever changed their own society or the world as a whole. Some were political or military leaders—kings, queens, presidents, generals, and the like—whose policies, conquests, or innovations reshaped the maps and futures of countries and entire continents. Among those falling into this category were the formidable Roman statesman/general Julius Caesar, who extended Rome's power into Gaul (what is now France); Caesar's lover and ally, the notorious Egyptian queen Cleopatra, who challenged the strongest male rulers of her day; and England's stalwart Queen Elizabeth I, whose defeat of the mighty Spanish Armada saved England from subjugation.

Some of history's other movers and shakers were scientists or other thinkers whose ideas and discoveries altered the way people conduct their everyday lives or view themselves and their place in nature. The electric light and other remarkable inventions of Thomas Edison, for example, revolutionized almost every aspect of home-life and the workplace; and the theories of naturalist Charles Darwin lit the way for biologists and other scientists in their ongoing efforts to understand the origins of living things, including human beings.

Still other people who made history were religious leaders and social reformers. The struggles of the Arabic prophet Muhammad more than a thousand years ago led to the establishment of one of the world's great religions—Islam; and the efforts and personal sacrifices of an American reverend named Martin Luther King Jr. brought about major improvements in race relations and the justice system in the United States.

Each anthology in the People Who Made History series begins with an introductory essay that provides a general overview of the individual's life, times, and contributions. The group of essays that follow are chosen for their accessibility to a young adult audience and carefully edited in consideration of the reading and comprehension levels of that audience. Some of the essays are by noted historians, professors, and other experts. Others are excerpts from contemporary writings by or about the pivotal individual in question. To aid the reader in choosing the material of immediate interest or need, an annotated table of contents summarizes the article's main themes and insights.

Each volume also contains extensive research tools, including a collection of excerpts from primary source documents pertaining to the individual under discussion. The volumes are rounded out with an extensive bibliography and a comprehensive index.

Plutarch, the renowned first-century Greek biographer and moralist, crystallized the idea behind Greenhaven's People Who Made History when he said, "To be ignorant of the lives of the most celebrated men of past ages is to continue in a state of childhood all our days." Indeed, since it is people who make history, every modern nation, organization, institution, invention, artifact, and idea is the result of the diligent efforts of one or more individuals, living or dead; and it is therefore impossible to understand how the world we live in came to be without examining the contributions of these individuals.

Introduction: From Rags to Religion

Malcolm X is often remembered as a religious crusader and a reformer of race issues. But there were more sides to this complex man than that. Malcolm was a hustler in his teen years, and later in life he exhibited a fanatical side that rebelled against such comparatively conservative civil rights reformers as Martin Luther King Jr. For Malcolm X, life was a struggle between these facets of his personality. In addition to his inner conflict, Malcolm had to contend with a country in which racial identification was in debate but racism was a certainty. African Americans faced persecution, poverty, poor education opportunities, and menial job prospects. Malcolm, like many other disillusioned black men, fell into the grim crime-ridden life that infested places like Harlem, New York. The only escape for a poor black man was protest, and protest came in many guises. Among the most radical of these was the Nation of Islam, a brotherhood of the Muslim faith. The Nation, as it was called, was a fast-growing underground movement of protest and revolution that drew in followers from all over the United States.

Some of the black men and women who joined this movement did so as soon as they had the opportunity. For Malcolm X, who became one of the Nation's most influential leaders, the path toward enlightenment was a much longer and more troubled one. Malcolm suffered the woes that only poverty and a life in the slums can offer. He endured the hardships of being an African American boy in a racist school system. From there he moved to the trials of criminal life, addictions, a murky track record with women, and eventually imprisonment. It was only while in prison that he learned that there was more that a black man living in America could do to change his place in society.

Malcolm's revolutionary attitudes did not grow just out of his attention to the various Nation of Islam role models who guided him toward Muslim leadership when he was an adult. Malcolm's ideas were shaped at an early age. Earl Little, Malcolm's father, was a disciple and president of a branch of the Universal Negro Improvement Association (UNIA) in Michigan, an organization that served as a predecessor to the Nation of Islam. The UNIA emphasized pride in black culture as well as in African heritage. Earl's outward public pride in his race, however, had an underlying uncertain and fanatical quality to it. His own role model, Marcus Garvey, who started the UNIA, believed that the integration of whites and blacks in society was not only impossible but detrimental to blacks. Earl, whose own son Malcolm had very light skin and gave the appearance of being at least half-white from birth, was privately doubtful of how far to take the Garveyites' message. He eventually left his Omaha branch of the UNIA, claiming that his home had been besieged by torch-wielding Ku Klux Klan members. His wife, Louise, Malcolm's mother, later claimed the incident never happened.

Louise Little had her own problems and confrontations with issues of race, and it only got worse when her seventh child, Malcolm Little, was born in 1925. How to deal with Malcolm's unique light coloration was a mystery to her. Some days she would take a sponge and violently wipe down Malcolm, hoping to erase all traces of darkness on his skin. Most of the time, however, she would beat him if he was caught with any white kids, and made him sit outside to tan until he was darker. "I feel definitely that just as my father favored me for being lighter than the other children, my mother gave me more hell for the same reason," Malcolm wrote. "She went out of her way never to let me become afflicted with a sense of color-superiority."[1] Malcolm watched the changing attitudes of his parents with curiosity and a painful distaste toward all the problems brought on by race. One of Malcolm's biographers, Bruce Perry, speculates that Malcolm's childhood was essentially a nonstop struggle to find a way to satisfy the demands on him made by both parents. "He had neither parent's unqualified approval," writes Perry. "And there was no way he could satisfy their irreconcilable demands."[2]

SCHOOL AND GIRLS

Malcolm lashed back at the world that so often called into question his racial identity. His childhood rampage was only made worse by the continuing and heightened strife of his home life, which consisted of regular beatings from both his mother and father. Despite his anger, Malcolm was not a bully. If anything, he defended the underdog, and championed weaker children who were often picked on or ridiculed. The extent of his rebellion was to stand up for these unfortunates and for himself only when absolutely necessary.

Malcolm's first solution to his racial anxiety was to become the class clown. His foolishness and back talk earned him the hatred of his teachers. His attitude, however, was not confined to school. He became disrespectful toward women and defiant toward his own parents and other adults in his life.

Many of his white teachers were blatantly racist, and Malcolm, who appeared not quite white and not quite black either, often ended up with the brunt of various jokes and slander. "The one thing I didn't like about history class was that the teacher, Mr. Williams, was a great one for 'nigger' jokes," Malcolm wrote. "One day during my first week of school, I walked into the room and he started singing to the class, as a joke, 'Way down yonder in the cotton field, some folks say that a nigger won't steal.' Very funny."[3] Many people saw the worst in Malcolm. His fellow black students saw a kid whose color was in doubt, and his teachers saw a troublemaker who, to them, was bad for being black and worse for being antagonistic. Since he showed no particular respect for them, he got slapped on the knuckles with rulers, was made to hold huge stacks of books in the corner, and was often sent to the principal's office. The principal of his elementary school was particularly hateful toward blacks, and he used to whip Malcolm with a rubber hose.

Whenever Malcolm had female teachers who disciplined him, he would vent his frustrations on girls in his class during recess and after school. He would shove and pinch them, kick them and push them off the swings. Yet he was very attentive to one or two girls in his classes, particularly as he got older and entered middle school.

Throughout his early life, Malcolm struggled with how to handle girls. He liked to encourage friction between his male friends and the girls they were interested in. He enjoyed sitting back and observing the strife that ensued. When the first girl approached Malcolm, he was extremely awkward. He let her follow him around but insisted she walk behind him, not with him. He would spend an entire day with her and then pretend not to know her the next day and insist on sitting alone in the school cafeteria.

In the sixth grade Malcolm's situation got worse. He committed various acts of rebellion against a teacher he hated and then threatened violence if she ever touched him again. Malcolm was forced to repeat that grade because of such incidents.

Meanwhile, his mother became pregnant with an illegitimate child. Malcolm was outraged and, ironically, felt more alone in the world than ever after hearing the news. With pressures at school and home mounting, Malcolm strayed deeper into antisocial behavior. At age thirteen, he broke into a store, and for the first of many times, committed robbery.

A CAREER CRIMINAL

By the time he reached seventh grade, Malcolm had become an amateur boxer and fought the toughest kids in the neighborhood. He was the worst troublemaker in his class, and he had committed various petty thefts. His family, living in Lansing, Michigan, was torn apart by his mother's alleged indecency. Louise Little was institutionalized as a psychiatric patient after the pain of her dishonor overwhelmed her. Malcolm wanted to leave Lansing and put in his own request to be transferred to a juvenile home. He was hoping to be placed in a facility in one of the wealthier neighborhoods, such as Mason, Michigan. It was in these homes that the better-off misfits went, and Malcolm aspired to be among them, to learn from them. His wish was finally granted shortly after his fourteenth birthday.

While in Mason, Malcolm showed some promise. He entered into a deep friendship with his half-sister Ella, who was raised by his grandfather separate from Malcolm and lived in Roxbury, Massachusetts, near a relatively upscale area called simply the Hill. Malcolm traveled to Roxbury whenever he could to visit her.

After six months in the juvenile home, Malcolm was declared stable enough to transfer to Mason High School. There he soaked up the culture of both the blacks and the whites, and became a sort of chameleon, able to adapt himself to any clique. By the beginning of the 1940s, Malcolm seemed to be growing into an obedient brother and student, swept up for the moment by the allure of the Roxbury area.

Malcolm's rebellious side, however, reasserted itself quickly. In 1941, Malcolm moved to Roxbury to live with Ella. He started having parties with the rowdier crowd of teenagers, breaking things in Ella's home while she was gone. Malcolm refused to help her with chores, and he defied her efforts to introduce him to the cultured, friendly folks of Roxbury. He got his hair conked, a certain style that was popular among the jazz-listening teens of the 1940s. He also started visiting the seedier clubs in town and hanging out with the jazz musicians there. Before long, he fell into the lucrative business of hustling.

By the mid-1940s, Malcolm had left school and was moving from job to job, sometimes working for the railroad, other times unemployed and making money on the streets. Attracted to the dark but fascinating culture of Harlem, he moved to New York and began to prostitute himself to homosexual men. He also became an amateur drug dealer, addicted to a range of illegal substances available on the streets. The addictions left his finances devastated despite the profits of hustling: "All the thousands of dollars I'd handled, and *I* had nothing. Just satisfying my cocaine habit alone cost me about twenty dollars a day."[4]

With several reliable friends, Malcolm established a minor burglary ring. This was profitable for a short while, but eventually Malcolm became intentionally careless, tired of the dismal and immoral work of criminal life. He was caught and arrested in 1946 and sentenced to a harsh prison sentence to last eight to ten years.

WHILE IN PRISON

In February 1946, Malcolm Little entered the Charlestown Prison. He was not yet twenty-one years old. Within the prison system, Malcolm was reborn. When he first came to the prison, he was boastful of his independent accomplishments as a criminal and a hustler. He entertained fellow inmates with stories of some of his better heists. Bruce Perry writes, "Prisoners enjoyed Malcolm's entertaining exaggerations, just as the crowds who later flocked to hear him speak did. He boasted what a big-time hood he had been and how many women he had conquered."[5] Malcolm planned to enjoy prison as much as he could, relish in the escape from the hustling world of Harlem, then return and begin again, refreshed. But eventually, a combination of boredom and a desire to be a smarter criminal drove him to read. He read everything he could get his hands on: literature, newspapers, political pamphlets. He met and befriended a fellow inmate named Bembry, a surprisingly well-read and well-educated man who had the ability to argue endlessly with Malcolm over any piece of literature available. Malcolm also debated religion sometimes, and arrived at the same conclusion for himself after every discussion: that religion was worthless.

Over the next few years, Malcolm went through a short series of transfers from one prison to the next, and finally ended up in Norfolk on the request of his family. It was one of the few prisons that allowed Malcolm's brothers and sisters to visit him. During these visits he learned that virtually his entire family, including Ella, had converted to a cause known as the Nation of Islam, a brotherhood of black men and women believing in a combination of the Muslim faith and black pride. They urged Malcolm to contact the Nation's leader, Elijah Muhammad. With his own loss of faith, Malcolm initially rejected their urgings, but he became fascinated with the Nation's argument that convicts such as he were victims of society and that it was not the black lawbreaker who should be blamed but, rather, the whites who had allegedly made him turn to crime. The Nation also gave him hope when nothing else would, and broke him out of his depressed fatalist state, promising to him and all the black people of the United States a way out of the slums of places like Harlem. Malcolm had decided while in prison that he abhorred the idea of returning to Harlem upon release. By 1949, Malcolm was a convert to the new faith.

Malcolm spent the rest of his prison sentence completing his education, learning all there was to learn about Elijah Muhammad and the Nation of Islam, and spreading the word to his fellow inmates. Most notably, he explored a facet of the Nation's teachings known as "the true knowledge." His family wrote him letters to help him better understand these teachings. "What they termed 'the true knowledge of the black man' that was possessed by the followers of The Honorable Elijah Muhammad was given shape for me in their lengthy letters." Malcolm explains this perhaps most important philosophy of the Black Muslim faith in his autobiography:

> "The true knowledge," reconstructed much more briefly than
> I received it, was that history had been "whitened" in the

white man's history books, and that the black man had been "brainwashed for hundreds of years.". . . . The slavemaster injected his Christian religion into this "Negro." This "Negro" was taught to worship an alien God having the same blond hair, pale skin, and blue eyes as the slavemaster. . . . This white man's Christian religion further deceived and brainwashed this "Negro" to always turn the other cheek, and grin, and scrape, and bow, and be humble, and to sing, and to pray, and to take whatever was dished out by the devilish white man.[6]

The Nation of Islam was designed to be the escape from this humbleness, the way out for the black man of America. Its theories were "the themes that would be most central to Black nationalism during that period—opposition to integration, self-defense, black capitalism, and racial pride."[7] Malcolm felt a pull to this philosophy not just because of his skin color but because of his past as well. "The very enormity of my previous life's guilt," he writes, "prepared me to accept the truth."[8]

By 1952, the year of his release from prison, Malcolm considered himself a changed man. He was wiser, more educated, and now a profound believer in the half-religious, half-political movement that was the new Islamic faith. Malcolm became a model prisoner and worked hard to get himself released early. By the time he got out, he was twenty-seven years old, and bursting with new ideas on how to spread the Nation's teachings.

BACK IN THE GHETTO

To begin his missionary work, Malcolm moved to Detroit, Michigan. There he attended meetings at Detroit's Temple Number One, established by Elijah Muhammad himself. Malcolm listened to Elijah speak Garvey-like sentiments regarding black separation from the white population. According to Elijah, white people were the devil and had no place in the new life of the black American. Malcolm was initiated into the Black Muslim movement while in Detroit, and from there he traveled from city to city spreading the good word of the Nation of Islam. Throughout the early 1950s, he toured Lansing and Flint, then left Michigan for Boston and New York City. In 1953 he was given the title of assistant minister for his contributions. Malcolm looked to Elijah Muhammad as a father; he let the memory of Earl Little's beatings and his troubled past fade away as much as possible. Elijah encouraged this by calling Malcolm a son.

Malcolm Little, then, took on his Nation name and became Malcolm X.

Malcolm was a true sufferer for his cause in these days. While touring, he lived on very little money. He was under-fed and undernourished, and stayed in the poorest areas of town. His love life was troubled. He became intimate with two women, Gloria (a figure from his past) and Heather. He tried to wed twice; the second time, he backed out of it and left Heather in Boston without even saying good-bye. The Is-lam faith consumed him, and he became a man of impor-tance second only to Elijah.

Elijah, meanwhile, was violating his own preachings in many ways. While Malcolm suffered, Elijah had several af-fairs behind his wife's back. Elijah continually violated the principles of the Nation of Islam by engaging in drinking, drugs, and other vices. Malcolm was unaware of these faults for many years, and throughout the 1950s he continued to act as a second voice of Elijah Muhammad, even traveling to other countries on Elijah's behalf.

Malcolm got his first hint of the dark side of Elijah Muhammad in 1954 when he replaced a local minister in New York who had been dismissed from the temple there by Elijah himself. The cause seemed to be an argument be-tween the minister and Elijah Muhammad. The minister, Elijah had said, was not disciplining his wife enough (i.e., through beatings and physical punishment) and should show his dominance or else divorce her. The minister did not want a divorce, nor did he wish to discipline his wife, so Elijah summarily ejected him from the Nation. Malcolm was only slightly troubled by the event. His faith in Elijah and his comfortable role as a son to him kept Malcolm more or less blind to his leader's weaknesses.

BOTH ORDER AND ANARCHY

Malcolm took over as Nation's head minister in New York, while Harlem continued to decay and sink deeper into a communal poverty. Malcolm X was ready to offer black Americans a better way of life. Fanatical promises were made. Malcolm wanted to take the black people on his imag-ined spaceships to a new Earth where the white man no longer dominated. He believed that most of what had kept the black man down was due to white people. The alterna-tive was to first segregate the blacks from the whites; then his people would naturally ascend to world dominance, which he believed was their destiny. Malcolm claimed that whites would become the new slaves in the future. These ideas gave hope to Nation followers, and the optimistic rhetoric drew many new members to the Black Muslims.

As a new chief minister, Malcolm honed and perfected his public speaking skills. His abilities came to rival those of Martin Luther King Jr., though his message to African Americans was different from King's. Whereas King preached the unity of blacks and whites in a peaceful, but equal, coexistence, Malcolm had no such lofty hopes for the world. The message of the Nation of Islam was the message of Malcolm X: Blacks were the superior race, and, after centuries of oppression, they would get what was due them very soon. King's rallies throughout the country were demonstrations of peace, attempts to coerce the government into change without violence. Malcolm's alternative was to offer power to the black community, the power to control their own destiny. While King restricted himself to peaceful methods, Malcolm's only rule was, in his own words, to utilize "any means necessary." "This is our motto," he told young civil rights fighters. "We reserve the right to use any means necessary to protect our humanity, or to make the world see that they respect us as human beings."[9] The inflammatory message, however, brought fear and suspicion from white authority, who believed armed insurrection was implied.

At first Malcolm's message was directed only to black men; his personal issues with women had not changed since his youth, and they made it awkward for him to figure out a place for women in the Nation of Islam. Nevertheless, Malcolm soon overcame some of his awkwardness with women and refined his speeches. In an effort to attract female converts, Malcolm said that black women were the most beautiful of all women and that the only way to defile a black woman or lessen her beauty was to force her in any way to imitate her white counterparts. The black woman was, according to Malcolm, the "queen mother" of the whole Earth.

In 1957, Malcolm was made the national representative of the Nation of Islam. He also took charge of a new Nation newspaper. His power was growing. When Malcolm criticized a fellow leader of the Nation, Elijah had that leader removed. When Malcolm wanted to build a new temple somewhere, or travel to any foreign land, he was given carte blanche. The only thing left for him to do on his own agenda was to marry.

Unfortunately, Malcolm's personal beliefs were still different than his public statements. Malcolm still felt deep down that women were inferior; he called them weak men, and he was particularly critical of bad mothers. The relationship between this attitude and his past family problems was obvious. His preoccupation with work helped him to stay away from the opposite sex for many years, but by 1958 the public, and his sister Ella, were beginning to frown upon Malcolm's conspicuous lack of family life. Every other major leader of the Nation had a wife, and people wondered why Malcolm X didn't too.

And so that year he married Betty Sanders, known in the Nation as simply "Bettye," a nurse and sister to a Black Muslim. The decision was based almost purely on logic and cold reasoning. He told his sister Ella that his marriage was inevitable, though not necessarily desired.

EXPANSION AND DOWNFALL

Now Malcolm had the respect of his people, a wife ready to serve the Nation with him, and all the resources he had ever asked for at his disposal. But events would soon embroil Malcolm and the Nation in controversy. A television documentary about the Black Muslim movement was produced in 1959. Titled *The Hate That Hate Produced*, the program brought the Nation of Islam to national attention. Controversial from its inception, the nongovernment-sponsored production was the first to acknowledge the existence of an organization that resisted integration of the races. Up until that point, many Americans were not aware that not all blacks were advocating a free and equal mixed-race society. In the words of historian Dean E. Robinson, the documentary "uncovered a black organization whose members had abandoned Christianity, rejected the goal of integration, and believed that white people were devils."[10]

Malcolm was spotlighted among other Nation leaders for the documentary. It portrayed him in a serious light, depicting him as an important leader in America whose words were having an effect on shaping race relations. Many blacks and whites got to hear Malcolm's message for the first time. Some were repelled by its angry insistence; others were attracted to its promise.

Reporters surround Malcolm X in 1964. Despite his popularity, he disliked the attention and devoted himself solely to spreading the beliefs of the Nation.

At the same time that Malcolm was making his biggest and most elaborate trips around the world to various third world countries, his wife was pregnant with his second daughter. The FBI and other government agents were keeping tabs on Malcolm and his family, tapping his phone lines and showing up to Nation rallies. Publicly, Malcolm was more confident and assertive than ever, but privately, he was under great stress due to the burdens of leadership and the invasion of his privacy. He did not like people watching him and was not interested in his own popularity. Many believed that he genuinely wanted only to spread his message, not be adored and given attention.

By the early 1960s, he began to lose steam, and a series of events set in motion a feeling on his part that the Nation was losing steam as well. In 1962 irrefutable evidence was made available to Malcolm of Elijah Muhammad's various indiscretions, including adultery. Malcolm quickly lost much of his respect for his adopted father. As leading Malcolm X historian Clayborne Carson puts it, "Malcolm's disillusionment with Elijah Muhammad resulted not only from political differences but also his personal dismay."[11] Then in 1963 Malcolm became upset over the largest civil rights march on Washington to date. After the event he said he could not understand why black people were so excited over a demonstration that he believed was run by whites, in front of a statue of a president "who has been dead for a hundred years and who didn't like us when he was alive."[12] He was angry over what he saw as the increasing ineffectualness of these types of easily controlled, police-observed demonstrations.

Meanwhile, the Nation of Islam itself had become a huge machine, creating a larger and larger membership. It had developed the attributes of a mass movement, and the money being donated to this movement was more than anyone could keep track of or calculate. White reporters were now allowed at Nation of Islam rallies, and soon almost anyone could come to see these events. Mobs often formed, and these became impossible for anyone to control, including Nation leaders.

For a while Malcolm's internal anger helped to fuel the external anger of his people. His hatred of the white man and his belief in the superiority of blacks were only made more potent by the frustrations he felt over the surveillance of his life and the increasing scrutinizing of his home and family. He began to lash out. The civil rights advocates of more peaceful change, such as Martin Luther King Jr., Roy Wilkins, Whitney Young, and A. Philip Randolph, became Malcolm's enemies simply because they were not loyal to the Nation. Sports figures such as Jackie Robinson and Joe Louis, formerly idols in the eyes of a younger Malcolm, were now just more "stooges" for the white establishment because they were not interested in joining up with the Nation's cause. Under the teachings of the Nation and Malcolm himself, people like Martin Luther King Jr. were actually doing damage to the black man in America. King's passive teachings were interpreted by Malcolm and many Nation members as demonstrating weakness in the black race, and it was felt that, under King's ideals, whites would not be punished severely enough. These attacks were quickly incorporated into Malcolm's later speeches as a Nation of Islam representative.

THE MUSLIM MOSQUE

In the end, however, Malcolm's frustrations—at the FBI, at King, at the white police, and at Elijah Muhammad's indiscretions—had limits. His supposed dislike of the attitudes of Martin Luther King Jr. and other black leaders was secretly matched by a grudging admiration for their accomplishments. His trips overseas helped open his eyes to multiracial peace. During a pilgrimage to Mecca, for example, Malcolm "reported that seeing Muslims of all colors worshiping together caused him to reject the view that all whites were devils."[13] Because of his loyalty to the Nation's message—his own message that he preached for years—he worked hard to keep these feelings hidden. But by the mid-1960s there was clear evidence of political differences between him and his old leader, Elijah Muhammad.

Malcolm's revelations, compounded with his increasing dismay at Elijah's personal vices, became motive enough for Malcolm to think about a quiet exit from the Nation of Islam. He kept his desire to leave hidden, but his differences with Elijah were made public because of a growing tension between them and an inability to work well together. Officially, Malcolm continued to support Elijah's positions, but he tried to nudge the Nation in new directions, closer now to the teachings of people like Martin Luther King Jr. Elijah Muhammad was upset. He went to his followers and told them that Malcolm was betraying his principles. Nation members were torn by the news, and several suffered divided loyalties. Hoping to save the Nation's unity, Elijah's family turned against Malcolm.

Elijah's tactic to keep Malcolm from making changes in or dividing the Nation was to send Malcolm away. He made it mandatory that Malcolm take frequent trips to other parts of the world, usually as an ambassador representing the Nation to other countries or else on missions of religious exploration into Muslim lands. Malcolm spent increasing time in Cairo on the pretense of studying orthodox Islam. Malcolm understood this to be a form of banishment. Upon returning from one trip, Malcolm gave a speech at Yale in which he questioned whether Elijah Muhammad was really "a man from God." Such an accusation could not be tolerated. Malcolm was ready to leave the Nation, and Elijah Muhammad was ready to see him go. In late 1963, after the assassination of President John F. Kennedy, Malcolm was indefinitely suspended from the Nation of Islam on the pretense of having given a bad speech about the former president. Malcolm did not protest his expulsion.

It took very little time for Malcolm to assert his independence. He hastily assembled a new organization, the Muslim Mosque, Incorporated, recruiting those who were still loyal to him. His new campaign was somewhat more peaceful; he wanted many of the things that Martin Luther King Jr. had advocated, including black voter participation, a new black political party, and a general increase in the "Negros' political strength." He thought blacks could change the system from within, rather than the Nation's attitude of simply creating a new system for blacks only:

> I used to define Black nationalism as the idea that the Black man should control the economy of his community, the politics of his community, and so forth. But when I was in Africa in May, in Ghana, I was speaking with the Algerian ambassador. . . . When I told him that my political, social, and economic philosophy was Black nationalism, he asked me very frankly: Well, where did that leave him? Because he was white. . . . Where does that leave revolutionaries in Morocco, Egypt, Iraq, Mauritania? So he showed me where I was alienating people who were true revolutionaries dedicated to overturning the system of exploitation that exists on this earth.[14]

With this loss of the old Nation black-elitist sentiments came a gain for Malcolm spiritually. Malcolm wanted his Muslim Mosque to be an organization with more of a religious focus and less of a political agenda as compared with the Nation. "The Muslim Mosque, Inc. . . . is religious. Its aim is to create an atmosphere and facilities in which people who are interested in Islam can get a better understanding of Islam."[15]

BACK TO RAGS

The violence and the running from the law that dotted Malcolm's past would return to haunt him now. Despite his softened rhetoric, Malcolm found himself targeted by groups who wanted him out of the way. The FBI was still tapping his phones, following him down the street, and attending his speeches with guns placed visibly on their belts. And, of course, Nation leader Elijah Muhammad seemed to have his own motive for Malcolm's removal. Malcolm was undermining Elijah Muhammad's political and religious credentials. He was pulling members away from Elijah's camp.

Malcolm knew that he was under surveillance, and he even referred to himself often, and with a sort of whimsical calm, as a marked man. He suspected everyone was out to

Malcolm X and Martin Luther King Jr. await a press conference in 1964. Although he disagreed with King's passive teachings, Malcolm later embraced many of King's philosophies.

get him. "There is a conspiracy to kill me," he told the *New York Post*, "because the racists know that I now believe the only way to help the Black man in this country is unity among Black people and white people."[16] Hounded by distrustful whites and an embittered Nation of Islam, Malcolm felt he was doomed.

For a while, Malcolm managed a peaceful existence. His rallies were free of violence; his Muslim Mosque, already spreading throughout the East Coast, was steadily growing. Many people still thought of Malcolm as a great man and a holy icon despite his departure from the Nation. Throughout 1964, Malcolm worked hard on a new autobiography, which became a way to vent his anger toward the figures of his past. Everyone, from Earl and Louise Little, to his crime ring in Harlem, to Elijah Muhammad himself, received criticism in the autobiography. Malcolm's life, as it is portrayed in the book, seems like a roller coaster of strife and defeats. Though some argue that the autobiography is heavily exaggerated, it cannot be denied that Malcolm had come a long way.

In 1964 Malcolm visited Martin Luther King Jr. and engaged in a discussion with him after a news conference. It seemed that much of his dislike of King's attitudes had been contained or changed, though he still harbored disagreements and felt that white people had had the largest hand in holding the black man back.

Meanwhile, Malcolm's relationship with his wife and children was somewhat strained as a result of the many trips he made and his inability to spend sufficient time at home. Still he pressed on, and the new Malcolm X, now known by the name Malik El-Shabazz, had a successful year thanks to the continuing development of the Mosque.

THE BREAKING POINT

The peace and quiet, however, was short-lived. In the end there were so many people watching and waiting that Malcolm's own suspicions of being a marked man were shared by the general public of the United States. On the morning of February 14, 1965, Malcolm's house was firebombed. Suspects caught by police included Nation of Islam members. Malcolm's reaction was a paradox of outward calm and inward panic; he expected that his days were numbered, and felt agitation about it. But the fact that he had escaped the firebombing only increased his earnestness to get his new message out to as many people as he could.

On February 21, he held a major address at the Audubon Ballroom in New York. In attendance were many Nation of Islam members, government agents from the FBI, a host of reporters and press, and a huge general public turnout. The crowd was a sea of people, and security was difficult to maintain. It was tough to determine even how many people were actually in attendance. Malcolm had only just begun his address when several shots, in rapid succession, rang out from somewhere in the throng. Malcolm fell, and chaos ensued. He was rushed to the Columbia Presbyterian Hospital and pronounced dead on arrival.

Though the police on the scene seemed relatively sure that this was an internal Nation matter and that the blame was on Nation members, it was partially unclear to the public just how many organizations and people were involved in Malcolm's assassination. Several Nation of Islam members became lead suspects and were soon found to be in possession of the murder weapon. One of them was John Ali, among the first to turn against Malcolm when Malcolm left the Nation. But it was never proved that Ali or any of his cohorts were acting under Nation sanction.

Many, including Malcolm's family, felt that the white police, who conducted the investigation, were also not to be trusted. It was clear just by examining the FBI file on Malcolm X that the police and the government both had a hostile and racist attitude toward him and all of Malcolm's followers. They saw Malcolm as a fanatic, and they viewed him as a serious threat to national security. And then there was what Malcolm himself had said publicly just three days before his death:

> Since 1961 there has been a working agreement between Elijah Muhammad and his Black Muslims and the Klan and the White Citizens' Council. They are all interested in keeping the Black man segregated. . . . That's one of the reasons Elijah's people want to murder me. They're afraid the same organizing skills I used to make the Black Muslim movement what it was will be used against them.[17]

Malcolm had reason to believe (though not necessarily full proof) that his accusations were true. But still the question remained: Was this enough to add white involvement to the mix of causes of Malcolm's death? Was his death just the lashing out of betrayed Nation of Islam followers, or was it really a conspiracy on multiple fronts? Historians are still asking these questions. The assassination of Malcolm X is a hotly contested event, and there are still, to this day, opposing views on the subject.

Fortunately for the cause of black rights in America, Malcolm's legacy was potent, both immediately after his death and decades later. Historian Clayborne Carson discusses some of the ways in which the world continued to take notice of Malcolm X after 1965:

> After his death, Malcolm's views reached an even larger audience than during his life. *The Autobiography of Malcolm X* . . . became a bestselling book following its publication in 1965. During subsequent years other books appeared containing texts of many of his speeches. . . . His words and image also exerted a lasting influence on African-American popular culture, as evidenced in the hip-hop or rap music of the late twentieth century and in director Spike Lee's film biography, *Malcolm X*.[18]

Perhaps it is fitting that Malcolm's last days were so hard to understand, and that his philosophies and his life are still being pondered today. To many, nothing about Malcolm X is easy to unravel; his life and his beliefs were complicated. On one occasion, in his final days, he was overheard apologizing to a woman for raising his voice. It was a rare moment of sentimentality. The woman said she understood, and Malcolm responded slowly, "I wonder if anybody really understands."[19]

NOTES

1. Malcolm X and Alex Haley, *The Autobiography of Malcolm X.* New York: Ballantine Books, 1992, pp. 10–11.
2. Bruce Perry, *Malcolm: The Life of a Man Who Changed Black America.* Barrytown, NY: Station Hill Press, 1991, p. 5.
3. Malcolm X and Haley, *The Autobiography of Malcolm X*, p. 35.
4. Malcolm X and Haley, *The Autobiography of Malcolm X,* p. 161.
5. Perry, *Malcolm,* p. 106.
6. Malcolm X and Haley, *The Autobiography of Malcolm X,* p. 188.
7. Dean E. Robinson, *Black Nationalism in American Politics and Thought.* Cambridge, England: Cambridge University Press, 2001, p. 35.
8. Malcolm X and Haley, *The Autobiography of Malcolm X,* p. 189.
9. Quoted in Steve Clark, ed., *Malcolm X Talks to Young People.* New York: Pathfinder Press, 1991, p. 67.
10. Robinson, *Black Nationalism in American Politics and Thought,* p. 34.
11. Quoted in Mark Carnes, ed., *Invisible Giants: Fifty Americans Who Shaped the Nation but Missed the History Books.* New York: Oxford University Press, 2002, p. 192.
12. Quoted in Perry, *Malcolm,* p. 239.
13. Quoted in Carnes, *Invisible Giants,* p. 192.
14. Quoted in Clark, *Malcolm X Talks to Young People,* p. 85.
15. Quoted in Clark, *Malcolm X Talks to Young People,* p. 84.
16. Quoted in Steve Clark, ed., *February 1965: The Final Speeches.* New York: Pathfinder Press, 1992, p. 181.
17. Quoted in Clark, *February 1965,* pp. 181–82.
18. Quoted in Carnes, *Invisible Giants,* p. 194.
19. Malcolm X and Haley, *The Autobiography of Malcolm X*, p. 434.

CHAPTER 1

EARLY LIFE

MALCOLM X

Malcolm's Troubled Childhood

Bruce Perry

Bruce Perry is an academic who earned his graduate
degree at Harvard. He went on to get a doctorate at
the University of Pennsylvania and ended up teaching there for several years. In his later life he has
written books on political science and history, but
his crowning achievement is his in-depth research
on the life of Malcolm Little, known in his activist
period as Malcolm X. He began by publishing several articles about Malcolm in various scholarly
journals, and as his fascination for the historical figure grew he began interviewing friends of Malcolm
X, fellow ministers, old ex-schoolmates, and associates of the Little family. Out of all this research came
a publication of some of Malcolm's famous speeches,
which Perry edited. Later Perry wrote a book of his
own about Malcolm X, entitled simply *Malcolm*. This
selection is excerpted from the first few chapters of
Malcolm, in which Perry looks into the troubled
childhood and schooling of this famous activist and
religious icon.

Earl Little had great expectations for his forthcoming seventh child. According to a family tradition that sprang from
ancient legends ascribing magic power to the number seven,
the child would be blessed with the best attributes of the ancestral bloodline. It was destined for greatness, particularly
if it were male. In anticipation of the youngster's future
achievements, Earl's father wrote from his Georgia farm and
directed that the infant be named John, after himself.

The baby was born on May 19, 1925, in Omaha, Nebraska.
"It's a boy," Earl wired his parents. "But he's white, just like
mama!" The physical similarity between the newborn child

and his paternal grandmother went beyond skin color. His eyes, like hers, were blue-green. His ash-blonde hair was tinged with cinnamon; hers turned reddish in the summer sun. The similarities appalled his grandmother, who despised the white blood in her veins. Her dark-skinned husband wept. No "albino" would be named after him.

The baby was christened Malcolm by his mother Louisa, who had been raised on the Caribbean island of Grenada. . . .

Earl didn't tell Louisa he had walked out on his first wife and his first three children. Passing himself off as a widower, he married his West Indian girlfriend shortly after they met. But they did not have much in common. While Louisa had had five years of Anglican schooling, Earl was nearly illiterate. She needled him about his ignorance, which he tried to hide with pretensions of learning. They were constantly at odds.

With his new wife in tow, Earl drifted from job to job and city to city. From Montreal, the Littles went to Philadelphia, where they had their first child, Wilfred. Soon afterward, they moved to Omaha, where Louisa gave birth to Malcolm's older sister Hilda, his brother Philbert, and then Malcolm himself. Earl was a disciple of [black activist] Marcus Garvey and was elected president of the Omaha branch of Garvey's Universal Negro Improvement Association. Louisa also joined the UNIA, which emphasized that blacks should be proud of their blackness and their African heritage. It urged them to free themselves from their dependence on whites, economically and otherwise. Garvey taught that instead of integrating with whites, blacks should establish their own sovereign nation. His message was so uplifting that hundreds of thousands of American, Caribbean, and other blacks rallied to his cause. Some of them tried resettling in Africa. . . .

ALMOST WHITE

In Milwaukee, the next stop on Earl's itinerary, he continued playing a prominent role at UNIA gatherings. He also drove his touring car to distant towns and villages, propagating Garvey's teachings and organizing new UNIA chapters. In Indiana Harbor, Indiana, he was evidently met with such enthusiasm that he briefly served as president of that town's UNIA chapter, even though he apparently never lived there.

After Malcolm's brother Reginald was born in August 1927, the Littles trekked from Milwaukee to Abion, Michigan, where Earl's brother Jim bootlegged moonshine. When revenue agents caught up with Jim, Malcolm's father moved the family to the northwestern outskirts of Lansing, where Malcolm's younger sister Yvonne was born. The Littles purchased an aging two-story farmhouse in a semi-rural, all-white neighborhood.

By this time, Malcolm was nearly four. His reddish-blonde hair was so close-cropped it gave his head a roundish, pumpkin-shaped appearance. Though his skin had grown darker, it was still fair. The other children teased him about his "high yellow" appearance. They called him "Chink" and made fun of his bluish eyes, which seemed to change color like his mother's. "We called him a freak of nature," Yvonne recalled years later.

Malcolm's father was as dark as Malcolm was light. Though blacks who heard his crusading oratory thought he hated whites, his white neighbors had a different impression. He greeted them with smiles and gave them fresh, homegrown produce from his vegetable garden. Black acquaintances recall how he shunned them for white ones whenever he found it expedient to do so. And the son he paraded when the church deacons visited was Malcolm, his fair-skinned pride and joy. To the best of Malcolm's recollection, he was the only son his father ever took with him to the Garveyite gatherings where Earl vigorously championed the theme of black pride.

Malcolm's mother, whose American friends called her Louise, was also in conflict about color. Despite the way she extolled the ideal of black pride, she favored her lighter-skinned relatives and proudly insisted she was West Indian, not African-American. Her father, she said, was a white "prince" and plantation owner. She tried to comb the natural curl from her hair in order to make it resemble the hair of the white friends she boasted. Sometimes she scrubbed Malcolm's face and neck violently. "I can make him look almost white if I bathe him enough," she told her white neighbor Anna Stohrer. Anna felt that Louise considered Malcolm superior to her other children because of his light complexion.

But Malcolm felt otherwise, partly because his mother bent over backward to make sure he would not think his fair skin made him superior. She admonished him to get out of the house so that the sun would tan and darken his skin. He thought she favored the darker children, partly because his light skin, like hers, was a painful reminder of her illegitimacy. He felt he was her least favorite child.

Since Louise was so ambivalent about Malcolm's skin color, he could not please her any more than he could please his conflict-ridden father. He had neither parent's unqualified approval. And there was no way he could satisfy their irreconcilable demands.

PUNISHMENT AND RESISTANCE

Sometimes, Earl beat Louise. He was also brutal to his children. At the slightest pretext, he beat the older ones almost savagely. If one of them violated one of his rules, he grabbed the nearest child—which one didn't seem to matter—and whaled the daylights out of him. Frequently, he administered his beatings with a sapling or a belt. "You'll kill that child, Early," Louise occasionally protested. But she never intervened. She was as afraid of her husband as her young ones were. Even some of the neighbors' children dreaded Earl Little.

Malcolm was spared the brunt of his father's brutality. Years later, he attributed the favoritism to his light skin color. Most of the beatings he received were administered by his mother, who ruled her children with an iron hand, without visible evidence of affection. Like so many autocrats, she tyrannized them the way she had been tyrannized, not only by her husband, but also by Gertrude, Jupiter, and Mary Jane Langdon. Sometimes she used a strap on Malcolm. And at times she punished him with a switch that she made him choose himself. He would try to find one that would snap, but whenever he succeeded, his mother made him fetch another, stouter one. She could hit a boy so hard with the back of her hand that it made him feel as if his head had been split open.

In a partly successful effort to discourage his mother from whipping him, Malcolm protested her beatings loudly enough for the neighbors to hear. He also rebelled in other ways. He refused to let his mother, who was a fanatic about cleanliness, bathe him. He also resisted her attempts to send him outdoors, so that the sun would darken his skin. Yet indoors, he avoided getting too close to her; whenever possible, he stayed in a different part of the house, playing marbles or poring over picture books. He was habitually surly. At times, he refused to speak to his mother. On one occasion, he reproached her for being "all witchy." Clenching his little fists, he screamed, "I could kill you."

Malcolm was learning that verbal protest could achieve results. His mother began yielding to his persistent clamor for the buttered biscuits she impatiently denied her other, less demanding youngsters. Yet his position in the household remained precarious, not only because of Louise's ambivalence about his skin color, but also because his father's favoritism toward him bred resentment in the other children. . . .

Years later, when Malcolm became a public figure, he lauded his father, a "jackleg" (self-ordained) preacher who subsisted largely on the contributions he received for the "visitin' preachin'" that he did in various black churches. He had so many rules that it was hard for his children to remember them all. But according to people who knew him, he failed to observe them himself. In addition to being brutal to his wife and children, he was notoriously unfaithful to Louise—"a natural-born whoremonger," his friend Chester Jones called him. From childhood onward, Malcolm would have great difficulty trying to decide whether to follow the path of virtue his father preached or the path of vice he often practiced. . . .

HIS FATHER'S DEATH

In 1931, Wesley, Louise's seventh child (Earl's tenth), was born. During the same year, Malcolm began kindergarten at Pleasant Grove Elementary School. His teacher, Olive Hicks, was well liked by the Little family, even though she later acknowledged she was somewhat afraid of blacks.

One day late in September, Malcolm returned home from school to find his parents embroiled in one of their habitual arguments. His father was determined to make a feast of one of the rabbits they raised and sold for cash. But Louise objected, not only because they needed the money, but also because she opposed eating rabbit on religious grounds. Enraged, Earl snatched a rabbit from its pen, tore off its head with his bare hands, threw the bleeding carcass at Louise's feet, and stormed out of the house. . . .

Bedtime approached without any sign of Earl. Frantically, Malcolm's mother clutched her children. Several miles away, in the no-man's-land separating Lansing from East Lansing, Malcolm's father boarded an interurban trolley. He reached for his changepurse but couldn't find it. At the next stop, he left the vehicle, perhaps to look for the purse. About twelve minutes later, another streetcar came by. There were no streetlamps and the driver failed to see him in the gloom. Minutes later, Earl was discovered lying beside the tracks. . . . The state police were summoned and found him still conscious. He told Trooper Laurence Baril that he had returned to the car stop just as the trolley was passing by and had tried to board the moving vehicle. But he had missed the step and had fallen under the rear wheels.

Shortly thereafter, six-year-old Malcolm awoke to the sound of his mother's screams. Officer Baril and another patrolman were in the living room, trying to calm her. They took her to the emergency room of Sparrow Hospital, where doctors were unable to save her husband. Malcolm, who knew only what he was later told about his father's death, wasn't sure what to believe about its cause. From what he and other members of the family said, his friends got the feeling that Earl's death had been accidental. But as Malcolm grew older, he began leaning towards his mother's theory that her husband had been done in by whites. Malcolm's autobiography gives the impression that his father was assassinated for political reasons by white assailants who bashed in his skull and laid him across the trolley tracks. But Trooper Baril recalls that Earl's skull was not crushed. "If it had been," he says, "Mr. Little would not have been able to explain how his injury had occurred."

Years after the streetcar ran over Earl, Malcolm would contend that his father had been killed by the hooded, black-robed members of a white hate-group called the Black Legion. But the records of the Lansing police and the Michigan state police, as well as newspaper accounts and the recollections of several of Mr. Little's black contemporaries, leave considerable doubt about whether the Legion ever operated in the Lansing area. . . .

In 1931, when Malcolm was six, he would not talk about his father's death. Tyrannical as Earl Little had been, his absence, according to [Malcolm's brother] Reginald, left the children unprotected and afraid, without a strong, reassuring hand to take command. Malcolm refused to eat. When his mother asked him why, he replied that those who try to eat disappear and never return. He also had difficulty sleeping. "Only dead people stretch out," he declared. . . .

Burdened by seven children and insufficient education, Malcolm's mother never got the opportunity to use her intellectual capacity. She was determined that her young ones would not suffer the same fate. They would be successful—great lawyers or captains of industry. Her aspirations were apparently fueled by the success imperatives of American culture, as well as by those pervading the West Indian culture in which she had been raised.

Believing that she was acting in her children's best interest, Louise pushed them academically. She pushed them hard. Mistakes were not permitted. The perfection she demanded of her youngsters was similar to the perfection that one of her Grenadian teachers had required of her; when she made mistakes in spelling, he beat her. Sometimes, he lashed her bare legs with a strap.

A number of Malcolm's elementary school teachers were nearly as autocratic. One stern taskmaster habitually enforced classroom discipline with a ruler. One day, she decided to use it on Malcolm and his mischievous friend Ores Whitney, who had been exchanging messages via paper airplane. But when she tried to rap Ores's knuckles with the ruler, he drew back his hands so quickly that it struck her kneecap with a resounding smack. Furious, she stood both boys in separate corners and proceeded to stack books on their outstretched arms. Each time their arms collapsed from the resulting pain, she piled the books back on. The "lesson" lasted for nearly the entire class period.

Malcolm also had several confrontations with the school principal, Arthur Delamarter, who didn't like Catholics, blacks, or anyone else who was "different." Delamarter, whose detachable shirt collars never quite matched the color of his shirts, was so enamored of the prerogatives of his position that teachers who ventured to pass through doorways ahead of him were elbowed unceremoniously aside.

Like Malcolm's father, Delamarter demanded absolute adherence to a puritanical moral code, which he enforced with a stout rubber hose. Most of the pupils were petrified of him. He injured the tendons of one boy's neck and thrashed others for offenses they didn't commit. Malcolm was not the only pupil to emerge from his office fighting back tears. Nor was Louise Little the only mother who vainly remonstrated with the Pleasant Grove School Board about his brutality.

Malcolm's grades suffered. It was not because he lacked intellectual curiosity; on the contrary, he'd go to the rear of the classroom, select a book from the library shelf, and eagerly absorb its contents. But when work was assigned, he'd drag his feet. He'd doodle, daydream, and stare out the window. When teachers called on him, he frequently had no idea what the class was doing. Even when he paid attention, he often had trouble completing his work, for he tended to give up as soon as he encountered difficulty. Slouched in his seat, his long legs protruding from beneath his desk, he acted as if he cared nothing about academic achievement or about what his teachers thought of him. He seemed more interested in securing the attention he was not getting at home. If the teacher called on someone else when he had his hand raised, he'd make a scene. If the pupils formed a line, he'd elbow his way to its head. He was the first child inside the school building in the morning, the first outside at recess time, and the first to leave when school was dismissed in the afternoon. Perhaps his determination to be first at school had something to do with his feeling that he came last at home.

Malcolm's harried teachers, at least one of whom felt that he disliked women, tried dealing with him in various ways. They moved his seat in an attempt to isolate him from other troublemakers. They detained him after school. His fifth grade teacher tried pulling his hair but found it too short to grab. Malcolm revenged himself by pulling the pigtails of smaller, less powerful females. He squirted water into their faces at the drinking fountain, shoved them off swings, pinched them, and kicked their shins. . . .

Malcolm's second-semester sixth grade teacher had an exceptionally difficult time with him. According to one former colleague, she was not highly interested in teaching; she was primarily interested in the extra income it brought. Nor did she seem to have much sympathy for her students. She publicly ridiculed the penmanship of a pupil who had broken his writing arm and was experiencing difficulty learning how to write with the other.

Malcolm fought ridicule with ridicule. He played the role of class clown to the hilt, flailing his arms like a monkey and amusing his classmates at the teacher's expense. When the class turned to artwork (for which Malcolm displayed a flair despite low grades), he drew lewd caricatures of her. His classmates could scarcely contain themselves. . . .

DESPERATION

Malcolm's autobiography is as silent about these facts as it is about another crisis that came to a head during 1938 because his mother had become pregnant. By her church's austere standards, she was a hypocrite, as her husband had been.

Shunned by friends and neighbors, Mrs. Little, who had borne the stigma of illegitimacy so long herself, could not bear the additional scandal. She pulled down the window-shades and practically went into hiding, even from her children, who were apparently embarrassed by her condition. She sat alone in a corner in her rocking chair, talking to herself as if the other family members weren't there, lashing out at whichever youngster carelessly ventured within reach. The young ones, who had to fend for themselves, grew unkempt. The once tidy house became disheveled. Bedbugs invaded. Hilda, Malcolm's sister, had to prepare most of the food. As his last remaining parental anchor gradually gave way, a sense of dread began to overwhelm him.

Late one night, Malcolm woke Reginald, grabbed his father's hunting rifle, and led his younger brother to Levandowski's grocery, where the Littles bought most of the food they couldn't raise themselves. Sheathing his fist in a tattered burlap sack, Malcolm smashed a window and climbed into the store. The climb proved too much for Reginald, whose hernia caused him considerable pain. Malcolm decided to take him home. He stole nothing, not even an apple. According to Reginald, Malcolm's decision to break into the store was prompted, not by hunger, but by a need to do something—anything—to relieve the helplessness they both felt. It was not the last time he'd commit a desperate act of self-assertion in a desperate situation.

JUNIOR HIGH

In September 1938, Malcolm belatedly began seventh grade at Pleasant Grove School, which the neighborhood children attended up through eighth grade. Olive Roosenraad, the new principal, became his teacher. She was far better educated than most grade school teachers and was well regarded for her dedication and instructional ability. Yet she was stern and cold and insisted on academic perfection. Malcolm responded with the same passive resistance that had exasperated his mother and his previous teachers. He sat sullenly, as if he wanted to curse her but didn't dare. Each time Mrs. Roosenraad returned one of his incomplete papers with a "D" or "F," he grew more and more despondent. He seemed defeated by his previous semester's failure. He would not ask for assistance. Yet when Barbara Hyde, who sat directly be-hind him, volunteered her help, his chilly exterior vanished. He responded with warmth to her gentle touch. Barbara con-sidered Malcolm to be one of the kindest people she had ever met. Years later, she concluded that his learning difficulties had stemmed from a tendency to shut himself off from the women who had been trying to educate him. . . .

FOSTER CARE

Malcolm's ambivalence about leaving home was temporar-ily resolved by his expulsion from Pleasant Grove, which re-sulted in his transfer to West Junior High School in late Oc-tober 1938. The decision to send him there in the middle of the semester was apparently predicated upon the fact that West was the only school in Lansing with a sizable black en-rollment. Yet the change had little positive impact on Mal-colm, who looked neither black nor white. A loner, he mixed infrequently with pupils of either race.

The move to West Junior High was made possible by Ma-bel and Thornton Gohanna, who, for a fee, agreed to board Malcolm in their West Side home near the school. Malcolm later charged that the move was the first step in a plot by so-cial workers to separate the Little children from their failing mother and place them in foster homes. Surviving records indicate, however, that the decision to relocate Malcolm was not part of any such scheme. It was a short-term expedient designed primarily to enable him to continue his schooling without interruption. His accusations apparently reflected his own divided state of mind.

In many ways, Malcolm liked living at the Gohannas' bet-ter than living at home. Mrs. Gohanna, who had no children of her own, took in, fed, and housed everyone from homeless children to ex-cons. The neighborhood kids liked her; so did the adults. Malcolm seemed grateful to the Gohannas, but he appeared to have doubts about whether they really liked him. He dropped hints that living with them was not what it had been cracked up to be. One court record indicates that he got along with them "fairly well," but his stealing contin-ued. He also experienced recurrent headaches. There were disputed reports of conflict between Malcolm and the Go-hannas—conflict that may have stemmed from the fact that the Gohannas were straitlaced and sticklers for cleanliness. Moreover, Mrs. Gohanna snooped in her boarders' rooms—

a habit Malcolm, who kept things to himself, probably found hard to tolerate.

But the thing Malcolm evidently found most difficult to endure was the Gohannas' religious fervor. They nearly worked themselves into a frenzy at their "Holy Roller" church, which they required him to attend. He refused to criticize them openly for their religious zeal, asserting how nice they were and how much he liked them. Yet, as a rule, he had very little respect for religious people, perhaps because most of those he knew had not set a good example. . . .

On some weekends Malcolm visited home. He was glad when Big Boy or one of the Gohannas accompanied him, as it made the ordeal easier. His mother's ordeal was far greater. Her widow's pension had been terminated by county officials who were reportedly incensed by her refusal to disclose the identity of her new baby's father. Grimly, she stuck to her guns and martyred herself for her tall, dark-skinned lover, who abandoned her. . . .

On January 9, 1939, Louise was adjudged insane and formally committed to the Kalamazoo asylum. Three days later, his old friend and fellow classroom rebel Ores Whitney died of a cerebral hemorrhage. When Malcolm was told, he burst into tears. His whole world was coming apart. . . .

JUVENILE HOME

Malcolm was not expelled, as his autobiography maintains. He remained at West Junior High and managed to squeak through the seventh grade. Some time after the semester ended, he returned to his parentless home, where nineteen-year-old Wilfred was working himself to exhaustion in an effort to keep the family from starving. There was no time for fathering. The burden of cooking, washing, ironing, mending, house-cleaning, and caring for the younger children fell primarily upon sixteen-year-old Hilda, who had been changing diapers since she was nine. Malcolm's attitude toward his "second mother" was ambivalent. He expressed concern about the pressure she was under and said he loved her. Yet he left all the work to her. Moreover, he frequently disobeyed her, perhaps because she was so much like his mother. She nagged him about cleanliness and the need to excel in school. She was also dictatorial, according to Reginald. Like Louise, she told Malcolm to let the sun darken his skin. Nevertheless, Reginald got the feeling that Hilda secretly favored Malcolm because he was so light.

Malcolm slept at home very little that summer. When he did, he frequently asked Arlington Cooper or someone else to keep him company. It wasn't just the loneliness. No one at home cared about him, he told Maynard Allyn, a social worker who periodically dropped in. By mid-August, Malcolm decided he'd be better off elsewhere and asked Allyn if the Ingham County authorities would allow him to live in the county juvenile home, which was a refuge for neglected children as well as a way station for juvenile offenders who were likely candidates for reform school.

Allyn recommended that fourteen-year-old Malcolm be made a ward of the county court, placed on probation, and housed in the juvenile home. Judge John McClellan followed Allyn's recommendations and granted Malcolm's request. Malcolm shed no tears as he departed for the county seat of Mason, where the juvenile home was located. Despite his later assertion that his departure had been forced on him by white officials, he was only too glad to be leaving a home that was so beleaguered and devoid of love. . . .

When Malcolm arrived in Mason, he was given his own room—the first he had ever had. But the best thing about the Ingham County juvenile home was the jovial, buxom woman who ran it: Lois Swerlein. "Ma" Swerlein was big—bigger than her husband, and probably stronger. But her ability to control her youthful charges was only incidentally related to her bulk. Children respected her authority because she exercised it with wisdom and compassion. Almost invariably, they liked her.

Malcolm was no exception. The disciplined but undictatorial environment was just what he needed. His appetite improved and he put on weight. Mrs. Swerlein, whose friends affectionately called her "Mrs. Gold Dust" because she used lavish quantities of Gold Dust soap powder, was as fanatic about cleanliness as Malcolm's mother had initially been. Yet Malcolm took all the dusting, sweeping, and mopping in stride. With an eagerness that Louise and Hilda would have found hard to believe, he even volunteered for extra chores. . . .

THE CHAMELEON

Smiled on by those in charge at home, Malcolm lost his need to wage war against authority figures at school. He was respectful to his teachers and attentive in class. In his eighth grade class, he ranked third. (Years later, he told one writer that he had invariably ranked first.) His performance may have been partly due to the fact that Mrs. Swerlein wanted him to do well in school, but it was chiefly due to his ability. When his English teacher called on him to recite a theme he had neglected to prepare at home, he stood, looked down at his notebook, and began reciting. Few, if any, of his classmates realized he was ad-libbing from a perfectly blank page.

Since Malcolm was the only eighth grade student who was black, some of his teachers tried hard to make him feel comfortable. But others created obstacles. His history teacher, Otto Grein, welcomed him to class one day by singing, "Way down yonder in the cotton field, some folks say that a nigger won't steal." African feet were so large, Mr. Grein asserted, that they leave holes in the ground. Malcolm, whose feet were large, got the message. Some of his classmates noticed, however, that Mr. Grein's feet were equally large.

"Little Malcolm"—his classmates teased him about his height—dealt with such people as best as he could. He became so adept at making friends that, with Mrs. Swerlein's backing, he was soon "tight" with many members of Mason's youthful upper crust. One friend was the daughter of one of the owners of the town's Chevrolet agency. Another was the son of a bank president. Malcolm became such a good politician that he was elected class president the second semester. He could hardly believe it. He attributed his election to his good grades and his pinkish, non-African appearance. The grades, however, had nothing to do with it. The reason he was so popular was that most of his classmates liked him. But he didn't seem to realize it, perhaps because he had felt unloved for so long. . . .

Malcolm exercised his growing authority in school. Periodically, the student body assembled in the auditorium. A teacher was posted in the balcony, where Malcolm's class sat. Malcolm asserted there was no need to station a teacher there to keep order. He said he'd do it himself—and he did. His authority was respected. . . .

When Malcolm visited Lansing on weekends, he transformed himself, like a chameleon, to fit into his non-white surroundings. He tailored his behavior to the demands of each color-conscious environment in other ways. For instance, among serious-minded blacks—the ones he seemed to respect—he talked about things that mattered. Among low-lives, he spoke gutter-talk and acted as if he had seduced every white girl in Mason. On one occasion, he dramatized the point by taking a condom out of his pocket and explaining his preference for the lubricated variety. He also participated peripherally in an incident in which a white woman was molested on the street by a number of older black youths. He seemed easily led by such boys, whom he openly envied and imitated. Conversely, younger boys sought his leadership, as did boys his age.

Malcolm was not as successful a politician in Lansing as he was in Mason. The West Side boys called him "Red." The label apparently infuriated Malcolm, who seemed to prefer the nickname "Harpy," which apparently alluded to the fact that he was constantly harping, or mouthing off, about something. . . .

Indeed, he was unwanted by many of Lansing's blacks, particularly those who aspired to middle-class status and looked down on Malcolm because of his poverty and his West Indian background. They wanted their daughters to go with "respectable" boys. But Malcolm's penchant for stealing, his father's unsavory reputation, and his mother's mental illness excluded him from such ranks. He was no more accepted by Lansing's blacks than he was by Mason's whites. At West Side parties, he stood around, watching others jitterbug, bob for apples, or spin the bottle. He was always on the edge of the crowd, a lonely-looking, uncommunicative, forgotten youngster.

Embracing Urban Black Culture

Douglas Henry Daniels

Douglas Henry Daniels is a popular biographer who
has written numerous works on the subject of black
studies and urban research. He has taught at the
University of California in Santa Barbara and has
written for the University of California Press. In the
Malcolm X tribute book *Malcolm X: Justice Seeker*,
he happily provides an alternative look at the teen
years of Malcolm's life, examining the cultural background of the young man and the kinds of influences
that jazz, dance, and clothing had on him. In this
essay he makes reference to the often-overlooked
closeness that Malcolm had to key cultural figures
of the early 1940s, including famous musicians such
as Duke Ellington. Malcolm's intimate relationship
with the culture of his teen years would serve to
strengthen his natural ability in adulthood to have
a finger on the pulse of black society.

In his youth Malcolm Little lindy-hopped to the swing bands
and associated with musicians, but writers have not discussed
this aspect of his adolescence. This is to some degree understandable. In the *Autobiography* Malcolm chronicled the
degradation of his early years followed by his imprisonment,
conversion, and abandonment of his life of crime, drugs, zoot
suits, processed hair, jazz, and jitterbugging. [To quote Malcolm himself,] "It was as though all of that life merely was
back there, without any remaining effect or influence.". . .

Close examination of his account of his adolescence,
however, reveals a pattern of continuity with his subsequent
development in terms of his constant evolution while remaining devoted to the values of northern Black urban culture. Such an appraisal is necessary to understand Malcolm,

Douglas Henry Daniels, "Schooling Malcolm: Malcolm Little and Black Culture During the Golden Age of Jazz," *Malcolm X: Justice Seeker*, edited by James B. Gwynne.
New York: Steppingstones Press, 1993. Copyright © 1993 by Steppingstones Press. Reproduced by permission.

for after all, one's formative years are linked to adult life. As Malcolm pointed out, "to understand [the life] of any person, his whole life, from birth, must be reviewed. All of our experiences fuse into our personality. Everything that ever happened to us is an ingredient.". . .

COOL CULTURE

Close reading of [Malcolm's] autobiography reveals a healthy cultural component to his adolescence which rarely receives attention. Malcolm presented an ever-changing identity in his development to emphasize his increasing sophistication and acquisition of Black cultural values. Significantly, his growth was encouraged by the constant counseling and coaching on the part of older and wiser Afro-Americans. The cool or hip philosophy that he learned accompanied his love of jazz music and dance in addition to the hustler activities for which he is chiefly known.

Despite changes in his identity and behavior, Malcolm's preference for jazz in the autobiography served to legitimate him with those urban dwellers who respected Black people and culture. Then too, it was a part of his demystification of the leadership of Negroes who aped the white elite and upheld its cultural values.

Young Malcolm's fascination with Roxbury and Harlem night life needs to be seen in light of his geographic origins and early social life. In Michigan he never had the opportunity to live with large numbers of Afro-Americans or experience Black urban culture. After the death of his father, the family was primarily concerned with putting food on the table and staying together. When the family was separated, Malcolm lived with whites and attended school with them. When he left Michigan, he "couldn't dance a lick"—an indication of his lack of exposure to Black culture.

From the time he arrived in Boston to live with his sister, Ella, Malcolm was primarily involved with Afro-Americans and their urban culture. His account of Boston and New York reflects a fascination with Black urban life as well as his naivete about the varieties of culture and class in Afro-America. The newcomer explained why he joined the society of poolroom attendants, shoeshine boys, numbers runners, waiters, and hustlers, people who idolized him after he became a race leader.

In the summer of 1940, Malcolm felt and appeared to his

sister as "country." Like other newcomers, he set about changing himself to appear hip and cool—the first in what was to be a series of attempts to rid himself of an embarrassing past and keep in step with contemporary trends throughout his life. One obvious route to follow was that of the Hill elite, the Black residents of Roxbury who "acted and lived differently from any Black people I'd dreamed of." They felt they were "cultured," "cultivated," and "dignified." The Hill people often owned homes and claimed they were professionals, "in government," "in finance," or "in law." They strode about "as if they were wearing top hats and cutaways.". . .

Although his sister preferred that he associate with them, Malcolm quickly concluded these were pretenders to status and high social position. Actually, the New England natives, the West Indians, and the descendants of the southern urban elite may very well have behaved in a manner that to them was natural. Such considerations never entered Malcolm's mind. He lumped New Englanders together with the "Southern strivers and scramblers" and West Indians, viewing them as "big-city" versions of bootblacks, janitors, cooks and maids he had seen in Lansing. He was amazed as much at their self-delusion as he was at their social snobbery. . . .

Instead he sought out the people whose status depended upon their own efforts in music, dance, sport, and hustling, and whose domain was within Black institutions such as restaurants, pool halls, bars, swing bands, and dance halls. Their behavior was rooted in Black cultural values that numerous Southern migrants and urban dwellers held dear. . . .

Malcolm's concern for natural behavior and manners reflected differences in style between the elite and other urban dwellers. The style in which Malcolm felt most comfortable was that of large numbers of poorer Blacks, recent migrants to cities, and hustlers, many of whom were united by their philosophy of cool and love of jazz and blues. While Malcolm rejected the Hill dwellers as pretentious, certainly pool players and loungers, racketeers, and card sharps are no more free of pretense and desires for higher status than anyone else. Nor was there anything natural about the zoot suit or conk hair style, both of which Malcolm eventually rejected.

Most significantly, it was these people, not the Hill dwellers, who befriended Malcolm, introduced him to their philosophy, put him at ease, counseled him, and claimed him as one of their own. Malcolm never forgot this, and it was part of the reason he was always their hero, before and after jail and, for that matter, in and out of the Nation of Islam. . . .

THE PHILOSOPHY OF COOL

Malcolm's increasing knowledge and exposure to Black cultural traditions found expression in the philosophy of cool that pervaded urban Afro-America. This aspect of Black culture has been traced to West African societies, where it functioned as an aesthetic and as a kind of philosophy useful for reconciling conflict. To be cool is to be self-possessed and in a state of equilibrium. It means avoiding the extremes of excitement and hot-headedness, on the one hand, and insensibility or immobility, on the other. One who has coolness can thus be a mediator and have a quieting, calming influence in society. . . .

By learning to be calm and collected, Malcolm prevented trouble. During two close calls with the police, he used his head, flagging them down to ask for directions when they were seen approaching. The police assumed a criminal would never be so bold or so calculated as to approach the police if he had just committed a crime. When he set up the burglary ring, Malcolm took command by pretending to be crazy enough to risk his life before the gang's very eyes. He played Russian roulette, telling them the leader could not be someone who was afraid of death, but they did not know he had palmed the single bullet instead of putting it into the chamber. During his period as a follower of Elijah Muhammad, Malcolm's intemperate statements resulted in his suspension from public speaking engagements. His last words shortly before his assassination, significantly, showed how self-possessed he could be despite the frustrations of his last few weeks. An altercation that the assassins staged to divert attention was greeted with Malcolm's statement, "'Hold it! Hold it! Don't get excited . . . Let's cool it, brothers—'". . .

After finding a job and before learning the more profound lessons of his new companions, Malcolm acquired the superficial aspects of the urban culture. These were the zoot suit, conk hair style, drug habits, and gambling. Zoot suits were the rage among Blacks in the cities, poorer whites in the immigrant districts, and Mexican-Americans in the southwest during the early forties. For Malcolm as well as other youth, it was a sign one had "arrived," that he was "cool." His new status had to be displayed publicly. Showing the suit off to its best advantage was known as "'cooling it'—hat dangled, knees close together, feet wide apart, both index fingers jabbed toward the floor." Malcolm learned "the long coat and swinging chain and the Punjab pants were much more dramatic if you stood that way." Proud of his new status as symbolized by the suit, he had himself photographed in this stance and sent copies airmail to Michigan. . . .

Malcolm learned to manipulate people through dress codes as he became increasingly sophisticated. When he received his draft notice, he "dragged out the wildest zoot suit in New York" and started to act crazy. He appeared at the induction center "costumed like an actor" and talking jive to officers and the psychiatrist. Later he felt his brother, Reginald, whom Malcolm introduced to New York night life, needed to dress more conservatively. So Malcolm presented him with an overcoat and a suit with the message he himself had learned: "In order to get something you had to look as though you already had something." While probably not adopted to mold opinion, Malcolm's wearing of the African shirts and Astrakhan cap of Black nationalists in the sixties reflected a concern with style that was meaningful to Afro-Americans. . . .

[While taking a] job on the railroad, Malcolm had the opportunity to go to the citadel of Black culture at the time, which was Harlem. He visited Small's Paradise, which had a show, but this was not enough. Before the night was over he included the Apollo and the Savoy in his rounds. Malcolm was overwhelmed. The young dance fan "had never seen such feverheat dancing." "In one night . . . Harlem—had just about narcotized me." He eventually moved out of Boston to be closer to the music and dance which increasingly figured in his life.

Working as a reefer peddler, Malcolm traveled with the swing bands, and he became more closely associated with the music and dance and his new heroes. Whenever he went to local dances, he would "show the country folks some plain and fancy lindy-hopping." His association with the musicians and their behavior was such that "in most cases," he was thought to be one of the band. Small town fans mobbed him for autographs, and in Buffalo, Malcolm claimed, his suit was nearly torn off. As a result of his travels and sales, Malcolm "became known to almost every popular Negro musician around New York in 1944–45."

Malcolm provided numerous examples of the recognition

he was accorded by well-known musicians. When he made a particularly sensational display of dancing, "even Duke Ellington half raised up from his piano stool and bowed" in salute. The only Black woman Malcolm dated in New York was a singer, and they went to hear Billie Holiday, who knew them. The entertainer sang Malcolm's song, "the one she knew I always liked so," and visited at their table. Malcolm's life had been threatened, and "Billie sensed something wrong with me." Moreover, she "knew that I was always high, but she knew me well enough to see that something else was wrong." Malcolm kept his distance, however, and his last mention of this event was when he claimed he had his picture taken with the two singers, huddled together with them at the table. . . .

Malcolm discovered greater humanity among the outcasts than among the so-called respectable citizens. He learned this when living in a building in which several prostitutes befriended him. "It was chiefly the women who weren't prostitutes who taught me to be very distrustful of most women; there seemed to be a higher code of ethics and sisterliness among those prostitutes than among numerous ladies of the church."

What is particularly striking about the early chapters is these bonds of friendship, trust, and humanity among people thought to be criminal or the victims of oppression. Despite the problems they faced as children and adults, Malcolm's family stuck by him in prison, introduced him to Islam, and provided for him in numerous ways. . . . The prostitutes with whom he lived treated Malcolm like a "kid brother.". . . And among the hustlers, there were people like the old-timer, Fewclothes, who maintained his dignity even though he depended on the charity of the people at Small's.

These examples of humanity and warmth among the poor and oppressed are not merely romanticizations of ghetto life or the good old days, as it was Malcolm's main desire to portray the pernicious effects of racism and ghetto life. The sordid decline of many of his hustler companions during his imprisonment probably stays with the average reader more than the bonds of friendship. Nonetheless, his ability to recall several instances of concern and caring is ample testimony to their impact on Malcolm and the fact that he valued them several years later. Despite the risks of ghetto life, there was a measure of security and solidarity in this Black urban world just as there was in the Nation of Islam later.

OPPORTUNITIES FOR CHANGE

Malcolm was in many ways a mirror or barometer of the changes Afro-American urbanites experienced from World War II to the sixties. Starting out as a country boy in the city, he was initiated into the popular as well as the superficial aspects of Black culture, learned to enlarge his limited opportunities through hustling and crime, and went through a remarkable spiritual conversion which enabled him to make a calculated analysis of the political arena from an international perspective. Initially, Black music provided the key to urban culture and to the homeboy's acceptance; then his display of sophistication in his hustles won him the respect he sought; later Islam, and finally Pan-Africanist thought provided paths of understanding. Malcolm's unique contribution to the process was his lending enormous popularity to each phase, swelling the ranks of the Black nationalists and the Pan-Africanists as he did the Muslims.

The changes in his identity brought into focus his singular ability to learn and, especially important, to benefit from the counsel and guidance of Afro-Americans—musicians, hustlers, Muslims, reporters, and politicians. Probably more than trained educators and scholars, these Afro-Americans contributed to Malcolm's growth and, ultimately, to the education of Black folk in the mid-twentieth century. Many educated people have difficulty understanding Malcolm's development and making a meaningful analysis of the Afro-American condition precisely because they lack a thorough grounding in Black culture, traditions, and experiences.

Outside observers have also misunderstood the emphasis on style in urban Afro-America. Malcolm, on the other hand, was aware of its connection with Afro-American aesthetics and traditions. He used his knowledge of styles of dress, for example, to popularize his ideals and perhaps to counter the pernicious effects of mass media. The zoot suit, the African national shirt, the conk, the afro and beard, the Astrakhan headgear after his trip overseas—every change signaled his changing ideals and growing sophistication.

Analyses of the role of culture in Malcolm's thought and growth invariably single out his statements concerning great African civilizations and the contributions of Islam and Arab culture. The popular music he discusses in his autobiography should help bring to the fore the importance of Afro-

American cultural traditions in his evolution. This phase of Black culture has its well-known dissidents; Charles "Yardbird" Parker is the classic example. Musicians who became Muslims in the forties were also rebels in the cultural domain if not in the political. These dissidents, though often they did not develop a sophisticated political analysis, were heralds of the cultural changes in popular music, dress, and use of drugs that underpinned the rebellion of the sixties. These musicians were Malcolm's first teachers, initiating him into Black cultural traditions which he subsequently developed through his readings in history.

In whatever phase we examine Malcolm, we find that he was a messenger spreading the gospel of Black culture. When he spoke as a minister, he used the idiom and folklore of his respective audiences, relying upon his intimate knowledge of the music world, the streets, prisons, small towns, and large cities. After prison when he returned to his old haunts to find his hustler friends, he relied on the wire—that rather singular legacy of the Black oral tradition—to locate others as well as street talk to communicate when he found them. His knowledge of the varieties of the Black vernacular and Afro-American culture enhanced his ability to reach audiences and popularize the content of his religious and political programs.

Malcolm also relied upon his close acquaintance with Black culture to criticize certain Negro political and social leaders and to validate his own analysis. He drew upon the folk and urban traditions and styles which initially had put him at ease and which did the same for his listeners, allowing him to instruct them once their guard had been lowered. He stressed the cultural pretensions of the Negro elite as he strove to teach Afro-Americans to respect their indigenous traditions. . . . Malcolm challenged the legitimacy of the Black elite, the traditional Negro professional class, and all those who wished to follow Euro-American cultural ideals. . . .

Malcolm's contributions to the Black cultural renaissance of the sixties are amply documented by a close reading of his autobiography. In the future he will perhaps win recognition for these insights as much as for his political analysis. In fact, it is very likely he would not have analyzed the American political system in the way that he did without his immersion in Black music and urban culture during his formative years.

A Life of Crime in Harlem

Louis A. DeCaro Jr.

Malcolm's upbringing in an unstable household, as well as his discipline problems and his fluctuating racial troubles in school, served to set the stage for a period of drugs, hustling, and criminal violence. After wandering from school to school, Malcolm finally ended up on the streets of New York City's Harlem, a dangerous place that bred criminal activity of the worst kind in the mid-1940s. It was here that Malcolm received a culture shock as he realized just how awful the state of the black American was at that time. Many people remember Malcolm X as the virtuous leader of the Nation of Islam who spent a lifetime devoted to religion and the aid of his fellow African Americans. But as Louis A. DeCaro Jr. points out, there was a time in Malcolm's young life when he, like many black Americans living in poverty in the '40s, turned to the demoralizing life of the New York City underworld. DeCaro, who has himself been an activist and writer for Harlem's Soul Release Prison Ministry and the Bethel Gospel Assembly, wrote extensively on the lives of black Americans past and present who grew up in New York City.

As Malcolm approached adolescence, conditions in the Little home worsened. Louise was unable to find or keep employment. Maybe this was because she was not only black but also the widow of a controversial black man who in death may have been even more disparaged by both whites and blacks. According to Malcolm, it was even rumored that Earl Little had committed suicide—a rumor the life insurance people gladly seized upon. Welfare assistance brought some relief, but it also introduced intrusive, racist welfare agents into their home.

Louise Little, who was a capable, independent Garveyite [follower of black activist Marcus Garvey], deeply resented the involvement of welfare agents in her domestic life. But Malcolm did not realize until later how important it was for his mother to maintain her pride, since pride "was just about all we had to preserve." However, by 1934, during the depth of the Great Depression, Malcolm's home life began visibly to fragment. Making every effort to keep her independence, Louise took in sewing and rented out garden space and even the dump that Earl had kept on the back of their property. She was fighting a losing battle, and it seems that her white neighbors made no significant effort to assist the fatherless Little family. Indeed, some may have been eager to see them leave. Wilfred recalled that somebody even shot their pet dog, just to give the Littles a "hard time." This period became the first phase of Malcolm's wayward years, the tragic detour his life would take on the road to religious activism. Ironically, however, it would be this same tragic detour that would lead Malcolm Little into the first moment of conversion. . . .

Life in Roxbury

Later, after Malcolm was transferred to a county-sponsored detention home in the largely white community of Mason, Michigan, he regularly had to attend a white church. He would later note that white people in that church "just sat and worshiped with words," while all the black people he had ever seen in church "threw their souls and bodies wholly into worship."

Malcolm had been transferred to the detention home because his behavior had worsened; but in Mason he tried to turn over a new leaf. According to his own account, he was well liked by the all-white staff of the detention home and his white classmates. On weekends he was allowed to spend time with his siblings in Lansing, but at the same time he also developed an interest in Lansing's lively black bars and nightclubs—foreshadowing his imminent transformation into a creature of the urban underworld.

Malcolm's experience in Mason then became increasingly bitter for him, particularly after he spent the summer of 1940 in Boston with his older half-sister, Ella. Free to explore the black world of Boston, he discovered that the jukebox clubs and other night spots in Lansing were nothing compared to the nightlife of Boston's black neighborhood, Roxbury. "I couldn't have feigned indifference if I had tried," Malcolm said. He was not simply impressed by the flashy nightlife, but by the experience of being within a vast black population for the first time. . . .

Ella enrolled Malcolm in an all-boys' school in Boston. He later recalled that when he saw that there were no girls in the class, he walked out and never set foot in a school again. He was also not impressed with the "Hill Negroes" of Roxbury—the upwardly mobile blacks whom he considered snooty, pretentious, and out of touch with the mass of Boston's black population. To Ella's disappointment, Malcolm preferred the "town ghetto section" which, to Malcolm, "seemed to hold a natural lure." . . .

Malcolm's closest friend in his Roxbury days, the musician Malcolm Jarvis, recalled that Malcolm always sought out the company of celebrities, and "always wanted to be next to famous and notorious people"—especially singers, musicians, and entertainers. According to Jarvis, Malcolm was seeking a sense of self-importance. "These feelings that he had about importance and being somebody in the world took place long before he landed in prison."

To many it might have seemed that Malcolm was seeking vicarious glory by associating with celebrities. But Jarvis seems to have realized that Malcolm's quest for recognition was deeply rooted in his life. Perhaps Malcolm, still immature and lacking in moral strength, had sought the importance he believed to be his destiny by pursuing the more earthy subculture of the hustler moving on the fringes of the entertainment world. . . .

THE MOVE TO HARLEM

Though Malcolm's life-style may have morally declined as he descended into the life of ghetto hustling, his race-consciousness remained intact. "I turned into a complete atheist," Malcolm would later recall of his days on the streets. This atheism was more practical than philosophical, convenient as it was to his emerging criminal life-style. Even so, it would prove to be fleeting. On the other hand, he never tried to shed his black consciousness: it was already too much a part of him. . . .

Malcolm wrote that from his early days in Lansing, he

had wanted to see Harlem, New York City's great center of black life and culture. Later on, when he lived in Boston, he would hear stories about "the Big Apple" from black musicians, merchant marines, and hustlers who had already visited the city. For Malcolm, however, Harlem was not just "the Big Apple," the glamorous haven for black musicians, celebrities, and hustlers. Harlem was also the heartbeat of Africa-in-America. For Malcolm, making the trip to Harlem was a kind of Garveyite pilgrimage, a way of reaffirming his belief in the black gospel that had been preached by his parents. "In fact," Malcolm reflected, "my father had described Harlem with pride, and showed us pictures of the huge parades by the Harlem followers of Marcus Garvey." . . .

When Malcolm arrived in New York City, eager to explore Harlem, it was not the glorious black Mecca it had been at the time of Garvey, or during the 1920s, when black painters, sculptors, poets, novelists and other creative individuals joined together in an artistic outpouring that was a self-announced cultural renaissance. When Malcolm arrived, probably in the summer of 1941, black New York in general was still recovering from the pangs of the Depression. . . .

Malcolm's ticket to Harlem came through a job he obtained on the New Haven Railroad, which ran along the eastern seaboard between Boston and Washington, D.C. He worked on the kitchen staff, serving food to passengers. However, for Malcolm, the job was only a way to reach Harlem. His employment record shows that he worked for the railroad three different times between 1941 and 1943, being discharged for insubordination at least once. One dining car waiter who worked with Malcolm later recalled: "At that time Malcolm's energy was not directed toward hard work. He was wild. He had only an eighth-grade education. I could have predicted he would eventually get into trouble."

Malcolm had discovered on one of his first jobs in Boston, working as a shoeshine in a dance hall, that "all you had to do was give white people a show and they'd buy anything you offered them." He found that, similarly, when he was selling sandwiches and other refreshments to white passengers, if he entertained and played up to them he would make plenty of sales. However, Malcolm apparently began to tire of "Uncle Tomming," as he called it. It seems, in fact, that the more familiar he became with Harlem and its environment, the less inclined he was to patronize white passengers.

Though Malcolm claimed to have had a politically "sterile mind" at that time, it is probably the case that being in Harlem increasingly sharpened his race-consciousness, just as his initial trip to Boston had done when he was still an adolescent living in Lansing. Thus, while he was seemingly oblivious to the message of the black Communists hawking copies of the *Daily Worker* in Harlem, he was not blind to the politics of race in the United States. His attitude toward white passengers became flip, and he began to flaunt himself as "an uncouth, wild young Negro," most likely to annoy the white passengers. "I'd even curse the customers," Malcolm later admitted. Malcolm had a particular dislike for white servicemen, for whom he would save his foulest language and sarcasm.

"It was inevitable that I was going to be fired sooner or later," Malcolm said, and eventually "an angry letter" from a passenger did get him fired. And though Malcolm was only about sixteen years old, he knew that because of his height he could again easily pass for an adult and acquire another job in the busy wartime economy. What really mattered to him was that he was in Harlem—which he described as being both "Seventh Heaven" and a narcotic for him.

ILLEGITIMATE WORK

In between his legitimate jobs, Malcolm was exploring the money-making possibilities of hustling. His autobiography gives vivid descriptions of accomplished hustlers, pimps, houses of prostitution, drug dealers, and other seamy sides of the Harlem underworld. Malcolm portrays himself as both a drug dealer and a "steerer"—the intermediary between prostitutes and their clients. However, while he illegally earned dollars playing these roles, he also became adept at gleaning financial support from women whose confidence he won.

At one woman's home, Malcolm would sit around and read "everything from Nick Carter thrillers to the Holy Bible"—an ironic glimpse that suggests that Malcolm was not entirely as "illiterate" as he would later portray his youth when representing the Nation: "I was a very wayward criminal, backward, illiterate, uneducated-type of person until I heard the teachings of the Honorable Elijah Muhammad."

Malcolm the hustler was not yet driven to scouring through volumes on philosophy, history, and religion, as he would later in prison. Discouraged and without motivation, Malcolm's intellectual flame was reduced to a flicker. His interest in the Bible was still an ineffective spark; his immatu-

DISTURBANCE IN HARLEM

Louis A. DeCaro Jr.'s writings on Malcolm's early life fall back on a traditional argument: that the tougher and more antagonistic elements of Malcolm's personality are almost entirely due to the harsh conditions of Harlem, the place in which Malcolm spent so many years. But just how bad was it? Historian Jervis Anderson puts the neighborhood in better perspective with a description of a typical riot in the depressing urban landscape of Malcolm's own 1940s Harlem.

The people dispersed through the streets and avenues, breaking store windows and spreading word that a white cop had shot and killed a black soldier, and thousands of other Harlemites poured out of their homes and joined the uprising. Business places were sacked, cars were overturned and set on fire, and policemen and firemen were stoned. During the rampage, Mayor Fiorello LaGuardia toured the streets in a sound truck, appealing for an end to the disorder, but scarcely anyone listened to him, even though in Harlem at that time he was the most respected and admired white New York political figure. Important black leaders came out to join in the appeal for calm, with no more success. One of them, Walter White, the executive secretary of the National Association for the Advancement of Colored People, said later that their pleas "were greeted with raucous shouts of disbelief, frequently couched in language as violent as the action of the window-smashers."

The disorder raged through the night, till sunrise on Monday. Very little then remained in most business places. Millions of dollars' worth of merchandise—furniture, rugs, bed linen, food, liquor, jewelry, clothing, cosmetics: almost everything that the looters were able to move—had been cleaned out and carried away. According to the Post, "clothes, dirty wash, canned goods, milk bottles, loaves of bread, and smashed liquor bottles littered the streets." Several hundred people were arrested—including youths who were strutting about in the top hats and tails they had stolen. Hundreds more were wounded—victims of police clubbing or shooting, or of lacerations they had suffered in forcing themselves through jagged openings in show windows. Adam Clayton Powell, Sr., said later that the riot was "the hottest hell ever created."

Jervis Anderson, *This Was Harlem: 1900–1950.* New York: Farrar, Straus, and Giroux, 1981.

rity and lack of discipline kept his reading diet limited to what he would later call "cowboy books." However, with his Garveyite background, his mother's good education and religious eclecticism, his religiously experienced notions of destiny, and his academic success in junior high school, Malcolm could never have been languishing in the kind of ignorance that typified the lives of the pushers, pimps, hustlers, and prostitutes with whom he associated. Malcolm himself acknowledged that the average hustler and criminal was "too uneducated to write a letter. I have known many slick, sharp-looking hustlers, who would have you think they had an interest in Wall Street; privately, they would get someone else to read a letter if they received one.". . .

Even more, Malcolm saw that Harlem was the white man's "sin-den" and "fleshpot," where black flesh was marketed for the satisfaction of whites. Moving in and through this "black-white nether world," Malcolm saw how race and sex mixed with business, and how the customers who could afford to pay for the use of black flesh were considered above repute within that netherworld. Malcolm had apparently been aware of the dynamics of interracial sex since his youth in Lansing, but in Harlem he saw those dynamics translated into a business. It is no wonder that Elijah Muhammad's ban on interracial relations—especially intermarriage—would later appeal to Malcolm. . . .

He inevitably came to believe that it was impossible for whites and blacks to respect each other as long as they interacted along the lines of the racial-sexual exploitation that has historically been a part of the white man's social order, ever since the days of slavery. Further, in looking back over these experiences in Harlem, Malcolm said he became suspicious of any white person who was "anxious to hang around Negroes, or to hang around in Negro communities.". . .

DETROIT RED

By the early 1940s, Malcolm Little was known as "Detroit Red," a streetwise young hustler who despite his height and good looks had to be differentiated from two other red-complexioned Harlemites with whom he shared the streets. The first was a professional armed robber who hailed from St. Louis and was thus tagged "St. Louis Red." The other, a friend of Malcolm's, was from Chicago, and bore the appropriate name, "Chicago Red." Malcolm preferred to identify himself by the best-known city of his home state, Detroit, rather than his hometown of Lansing. . . .

When Malcolm could not make money in independent endeavors, he might get temporary work, as he did at Jimmy's Chicken Shack in Harlem. He claims to have worked there briefly as a waiter, but [Malcolm's associate] Clarence Atkins suggested that Malcolm's affiliation with the restaurant was far more extensive—perhaps reflecting Malcolm's dependency in those days: "He was flunking for Jimmy . . . doing anything, like washing dishes, mopping floors, or whatever, you know . . . because he could eat, and Jimmy had a place upstairs over the place where he could sleep." Malcolm's prison file confirms that he worked at the popular Harlem restaurant for about two years, from 1942 through 1944, after which he returned to Boston. Rather than emphasizing his more extended, and perhaps humbling, dependency on Jimmy's Chicken Shack, it is interesting that Malcolm focused heavily on his job as a waiter at Small's Paradise, a famous Harlem nightspot.

Malcolm admitted that he did not work very long at Small's, and that he lost his job after he attempted to steer a customer to a prostitute—and the customer turned out to be a vice officer. However, Malcolm made Small's Paradise the centerpiece of his street schooling—the place where sophisticated, big-time hustlers taught him about a more urbane level of professional crime. It is not clear if Malcolm worked at Small's steadily or shifted between it and other jobs, both legal and otherwise. In any case, it is certain that he spent a great deal of time there.

For a while, Malcolm worked for a "downtown Jew," a nightclub entrepreneur whom he called "Hymie." According to Malcolm, he and Hymie got along pretty well, and Hymie was sympathetic to the black struggle in a racist society. For Hymie, Malcolm processed and delivered bootleg alcohol until the operation fell through. He wrote in his autobiography that he thought his Jewish boss had been killed under mysterious circumstances. However, it seems Hymie, whose real name was Abe Goldstein, was still alive by the time Malcolm was imprisoned in 1946. Goldstein remembered his young black assistant as being "a bit unstable and neurotic but under proper guidance, a good boy." Unfortunately, Goldstein had not been willing or able to give young Malcolm such proper guidance.

Another time, Malcolm created his own traveling drug dealership by using his old railroad employee I.D. to gain access to the train. With a large supply of marijuana, Malcolm moved throughout the East Coast, catering especially to the peripatetic jazz bands. He apparently enjoyed associating with these musicians, not only because he was a jazz enthusiast himself but because he undoubtedly hungered for the kind of public recognition they received. One senses a hint of pleasure in Malcolm's recollection that he was sometimes mobbed by jazz fans along with the band members. Even more, Malcolm enjoyed the success of his novel line of work: "Nobody had ever heard of a traveling reefer peddler."

MALCOLM THE CRIMINAL

Malcolm's evolution into an outlaw was steady, though, as Clarence Atkins said, "I'm sure that he was never no big time racketeer or thug." He dabbled in gambling, numbers, "little cons—little confidence games on people." Otherwise, he and his friend Sammy "Pretty Boy" McKnight would periodically burglarize one of Harlem's popular nightspots, such as LaFamille, and then divide the spoils. Through Sammy in particular, Malcolm seems to have customized his criminality. As Malcolm's closest friend in Harlem, it was apparently Sammy who encouraged him to specialize in peddling marijuana, as well as to snort cocaine—especially before committing armed robbery. In any case, according to Atkins, Sammy's apartment was probably the closest thing to a traditional home that Malcolm had in Harlem.

Atkins recalled that Malcolm and his associates would regularly gather at Sammy's apartment, often in a spontaneous "communion gathering," where Sammy would cook and where they would relax and smoke marijuana. This was perhaps the only family Malcolm knew when he was a hustler in Harlem. Typically, while some ate and fell asleep on the couch, or listened to the latest bebop records of Charlie Parker and Dizzy Gillespie, others frequently swapped their girlfriends for sexual relations. "Sammy would cook and we had music," Atkins recalled, "and there were always girls, always." It was probably one of the few secure moments at a time when Malcolm's life was otherwise essentially a continuous, and sometimes dangerous, street contest of "liberties and chances.". . .

Key to that perseverance, for Malcolm, was minimizing or

avoiding altogether the necessity of a full-time job, a jail sentence, or a term of service in the military. He had been able to keep full-time employment to a minimum by hustling and moving from job to job. He was also able to avoid going to jail. But in 1943 Malcolm received "Uncle Sam's greetings," which came to him in Harlem by way of his sister Ella in Boston. He was determined not to serve in the military—particularly not in wartime.

Malcolm agreed with his friend Shorty, and many other "ghetto Negroes," who objected to serving in the wartime military: "Whitey owns everything. He wants us to go and bleed for him? Let him fight." So when his draft notice came, Malcolm was determined to find a way not to serve. In his autobiography, he explained how he began to hustle extensively in the hope that his reputation would render him *persona non grata* in the eyes of the draft board. Malcolm, assuming that Harlem was filled with black army intelligence agents, began to make a public spectacle of himself—hoping to get their attention; he began "noising around" that he was a Japanese sympathizer and deliberately acted "high and crazy" in public places. . . .

According to Malcolm, he left Harlem in 1945 because he tired of living under the threats of criminals and police officers alike. Although there are some variations of Malcolm's account of this time, there is agreement that Malcolm left Harlem at a time of crisis. His associate Clarence Atkins suggests that while Malcolm may have been facing dismal circumstances, he and his friends gathered together on the night of his departure from Harlem. He recalled that none of Malcolm's Harlem friends wanted him to leave, leading Atkins to suspect that Malcolm was not in the kind of danger he portrayed in his autobiography. . . .

Probably persuaded by his Boston friends as much as by his bad luck in Harlem, Malcolm decided to return to Boston with his white woman and Jarvis. Perhaps high on drugs, he talked incessantly throughout the whole trip. His criminal career in Harlem ended, as it would also end in Boston— quite ingloriously, even by criminal standards. However, the next time Malcolm Little would come to Harlem, things would be different.

Waiting to Be Caught

Eugene Victor Wolfenstein

Malcolm's life as a fugitive from the white police eventually decayed into a drug-induced sleepless nightmare. His role models were actors in Hollywood movies and hustlers on the streets like himself. As Eugene Victor Wolfenstein describes in the following passage, Malcolm eventually became so distressed with the condition of his life that he became careless with his burglaries, in the hopes of getting caught intentionally. Even prison life began to seem better than what he had in New York. Wolfenstein's book *The Victims of Democracy* discusses some of the motives for Malcolm's carelessness as the leader of a burglary ring. As a professor of political science at the University of California Los Angeles, Dr. Wolfenstein's intellectual interests revolve around the psychoanalysis of historical figures like Malcolm X, Marx and Marxism, and the theories of Nietzsche. He has written several books on these subjects.

We now understand why Malcolm considered the United States to be a criminal society. Not only is the hustling society a logically determined and essential side of American capitalism, not only is the continued existence of this shadowy realm contingent upon the criminalization of black people who have been kept "oppressed, and deprived and ignorant, and unable to get decent jobs," but those people who have been driven to criminal activity are used to criminalize the image of all black people. And that, to use Malcolm's terms, is "tricky logic," a "con game," a "hustle."

Needless to say, Malcolm did not see either himself or his situation in this light during his own hustling period. He was mesmerized by the Harlem underworld, and he viewed himself as an heroic outlaw—an image that was reinforced not only by the Code but also by the movies. . . . Watching Bogart in action, Malcolm would project himself into the hero's role; when the action came to an end, he would introject the composite character thus formed. In this way Bogart became a white image of the black hero, and Malcolm in turn became a black incarnation of the white one. The movie experience was a form of hypnosis: the theater was a looking-glass world populated by fictionalized and highly erotized images of his past; the screen was a magic mirror in which he saw himself reflected larger than life. By suspending all disbelief in these shades and shadows, Malcolm emerged from the theater into the Harlem twilight as a cool, tough, and sensual young hustler who had risen above the antinomies of class, race, and morality.

Malcolm's transcendence of his situation was of course more fiction than fact. In reality he was falling below it, sinking into a nightmarish state of unconscious subjectivity. His successful and self-conscious practice of hustling . . . lasted only about two years. At the end of that time he was already beginning to lose control. . . . Malcolm was narcotizing himself into a "dream world" in order to escape from the insecurity and uncertainty of the real one. He was not unique in so doing: alcoholism and narcotics addiction are familiar ghetto diseases. Like gambling or the sexual "Game," they help one to forget the misery and shame of ghetto existence. But unlike these other escape mechanisms, they invade the mind physically. Numbing both conciousness and conscience, blurring the sharp edges of the objective world, they transport the user into a hazy realm of movies-come-to-life. . . .

Thus Malcolm was the victim of narcotization, just as he was of criminalization. There was a bourgeois interest realized in his loss of consciousness. Yet those interests, to be thus realized, had to be mediated by his individual motives, by the contradictory forces in his de-formed character. Malcolm was trying to escape from an internal as well as an external danger: the realistic anxiety of living in an objective state of war was magnified by the moral anxiety aroused by his unconscious sense of guilt. He was a haunted as well as a hunted man. . . .

HUNTED

The police were looking for him. It was "all over the wire" that he was armed and dangerous. Then he got into a fight with a "scared kid hustler," and there were some Italians looking for him, who thought he had "stuck up their crap game." "Everything was building up, closing in on me. I was trapped in so many cross turns." The drugs no longer helped, the paranoia that is the essential spirit of the hustling society was enveloping him in a phantasmagoric play of malign forces, half palpable, half insensible, and totally terrifying. But Malcolm did have one real friend in New York, Sammy the Pimp, who knew about his trouble. Sammy called [Malcolm's friend] Shorty in Boston to come collect Malcolm before he got killed. . . . Malcolm "didn't put up any objections to leaving." But "through just about the whole ride [to Boston], I talked out of my head."

Malcolm had been bloodied in the war of all against all, but he had not been bowed. He had been forced to beat a retreat, but he had not simply turned tail and run. He was, however, physically and mentally exhausted; his energy stores were completely depleted. For two weeks he slept, smoked marijuana, and slept some more. At the end of that time he connected for some cocaine; and with the "snow" producing its familiar feeling—"an illusion of supreme well-being and a soaring over-confidence in both physical and mental ability"—he gradually woke up. Then, "after about a month of 'laying dead,' as inactivity was called, I knew I had to get some kind of hustle going." . . .

For Malcolm, the circle of self-destructive aggressivity was almost closed: criminality from a sense of guilt, through the narcotic magnification of the hustling society's paranoid subjectivity, was resulting in what we may call *paranoid nihilism*, i.e., an impulsion toward killing and *therefore* being killed. Within this tightening circle, on this narrowing ground, Malcolm built an illusory life during his last months in Boston. . . . The progressive tendency in Malcolm's character had not been entirely destroyed; he was still struggling, although with diminishing strength as time passed, to be a success in life, to work and love as a free man.

THE RING

Malcolm sought to realize this ambition through the formation of a burglary ring. As we have seen, he knew he had to find a hustle; and he wanted to find one that would also liberate Shorty from the slavery of an underpaid musical career. Burglary had that potential. Moreover, "burglary, properly executed, though it had its dangers, offered the maximum chances of success at the minimum risk." Proper execution involved finding and "casing" good locations; the commission of the crime; and the disposal of the take. It was also necessary to specialize in the most suitable "category" of the "science." Finally, the ring itself had to be unbreakable—absolutely trustworthy and unquestioningly loyal to its "boss."

Keeping these lessons of his schooling in mind, Malcolm designed what he hoped would be the "perfect operation." The ring would consist of himself, Shorty, a friend of Shorty's who had wearied of the straight life, Sophia ([a white woman] with whom he was [repeatedly] deeply involved), and Sophia's younger sister, who shared Sophia's taste for black men and taboo pleasures. The particular area was to be nighttime house-burglary, with Shorty's friend and the two women as "finders," all three men as the actual thieves, and a smart, reliable fence to buy the merchandise. (Of course, Malcolm knew that "fences robbed burglars worse than the burglars robbed the victims"; but that was, it might be said, an unavoidable cost of running a small, competitive enterprise.) And he established himself as boss by faking a solitary game of Russian roulette: with his cohorts watching, he held a gun to his head and pulled the trigger, twice—after carefully palming the one bullet he had apparently left in the chamber. . . .

For some time thereafter, the burglary ring was an economic success. But the ring was not only the materialization of Malcolm's labor-power; it was also the embodiment of his emotional energies. As he put it, his robber gang was "like a family unit." Shorty had paired off with Sophia's sister, Malcolm and Sophia acted "as though we had been together for fifty years," and the other fellow was cool and congenial. There was thus a certain amount of group love and solidarity. But if the unit was like a family, it more nearly resembled a horde-family than a human one. Malcolm ruled over his subjects with a tyrannical hand, with a mixture of narcissistic authority and raw power. Moreover, he often terrorized Sophia. . . .

THE INEVITABLE CAPTURE

Malcolm and his robber band had been holding "hot" merchandise from the outset; the women had even worn some of the furs and jewelry in public. In time, one policeman or another would have noticed this conspicuous display and busted the ring. But Malcolm cut the process short by making the burglar's worst possible mistake: he took a stolen watch into a jewelry shop to be repaired! Not surprisingly, when he arrived to pick it up, the police were waiting. He paid for the watch, and "a fellow suddenly appeared from the back. . . . One hand was in his pocket. I knew he was a cop. He said, quietly, 'Step into the back.'" It was all over, the game had been played . . . but then:

> Just as I started back there, an innocent Negro walked into the shop. . . . The detective, thinking he was with me, turned to him.

> There I was, wearing my gun, and the detective talking to that Negro with his back to me. Today I believe Allah was with me even then. I didn't try to shoot him. And that saved my life. . . . I raised my arm, and motioned to him, "Here, take my gun."

Malcolm was disarmed—and then two other detectives appeared from the back: "They'd had me covered. One false move, I'd have been dead."

Allah, or at least his own moral character, did in truth save Malcolm: because he was unable to kill, he was not killed. The regressive unfolding of Malcolm's character thus did not reach its logical conclusion. This may be an adequate explanation of why he asked the detective to take the gun, but it does not explain why he made the mistake that set up the confrontation. The solution to that problem, however, lies close at hand. As any well-schooled hustler would say, by "thinking he could get away with it," Malcolm was "asking to be caught." He was, in the first place, breaking the law and defying his own conscience; his criminality was therefore immoral as well as illegal, but his actions were not irrational in and of themselves. . . . However, he was offending against consciousness as well as conscience. He was regressing into a phantasy world of infantile omnipotence, a dream world in which he could "get away with" anything. In reality, he was getting away with less and less; and as his criminality from a sense of guilt increasingly took on the character of paranoid nihilism, it was becoming quite likely that he would not even escape with his life. In his words, "I had gotten to the point where I was walking on my own coffin." And when the drugs were not beclouding his mind, he was painfully aware of this contradiction between phantasy and reality. He knew he was destroying himself, but there was nothing he could *choose* to do about it. . . .

In the present instance, he was asking the police to catch him and thereby bring to an end his participation in the war of all against all. Furthermore, if we view the regression of Malcolm's character from an extended temporal perspective, we recognize that its premise was his moral identification with his oppressor, i.e., his whitened-out conscience. It follows from this premise that his criminal actions were produced by and reproductive of an unconscious sense of guilt, and that paranoid nihilism followed in turn as the attempted narcotic negation of the unconscious negation of his conscious activity. This negation of the negation is clearly not an affirmation, but, rather, a retreat into madness, if not a plunge into the void of nonexistence. Short of this fatal conclusion, however, the premise remains determinative, so that the process of psychological regression entails an ever-increasing need for punishment. Thus we may conclude: in order to escape the maximum penalty of death, Malcolm was forced to accept the lesser one of imprisonment.

CHAPTER 2

IMPRISONMENT

MALCOLM X

From Criminal to Intellectual

William Strickland

Influences both within and outside the prison system convinced Malcolm that there was more to life than hustling and drugs. His family's adoption of the Islamic faith brought Malcolm a new religion and social philosophy. In addition, his sentence in Charlestown prison afforded him the time to educate himself and sharpen his intellectual skills. In the following selection from *Malcolm X: Make It Plain,* writer William Strickland discusses Malcolm's change in lifestyle, from criminal and hustler to reformed philosopher and thinker. *Make It Plain* is a very special documentary on Malcolm's life, including a wealth of photos of Malcolm at all stages in his life as well as comments from family members and friends. William Strickland himself met Malcolm on several occasions and has acted as a contributing editor for *Essence* magazine and the international journal *African World.*

Ella [Malcolm's half sister] was a revelation to Malcolm. He said that she was the first really *Black* person he had met who was proud of her dark complexion. (Did she remind him of the motto he had heard at the meetings his father sometimes took him to: "Up, you mighty race, you can accomplish what you will"?) At any rate, when Ella extended an invitation to visit her in Boston, Malcolm said he "jumped at it."

When Malcolm first came to Boston, in the summer of 1940, he was fifteen years old, a self-described "country hick from Mason, Michigan." The Black Roxbury neighborhood was, therefore, a revelation he found so exhilarating and intoxicating that "I couldn't have feigned indifference if I had tried to. People talked casually about Chicago, Detroit, New York. I didn't know the world contained as many Negroes as I saw thronging downtown Roxbury at night, especially on Saturdays. Neon lights, nightclubs, pool halls, bars, the cars they drove!"

Malcolm was hooked. When he returned to [his white foster home in] Mason, he wrote Ella "almost every day." He was "restless" with Mason and "with being around white people." Roxbury, the racial Mecca, had fired his blood beyond cooling. He had to return—like his father before him—to the flame. (He did not, of course, know that far away across the Atlantic, the man who had inspired his father and mother and who had made "Race!" a beacon that had thrilled so many— as it was now thrilling Malcolm—had died in London of a cerebral hemorrhage. Marcus Garvey was dead at fifty-three.)

A Hustler on the Move

By 1941, Ella had negotiated with the Michigan authorities to gain custody of Malcolm. She sent for him to come live with her, his half brother, Earl, Jr., and his half sister Mary in Ella's house on "the Hill" in Roxbury. Malcolm arrived but quickly deserted "the Hill" for the swinging nightlife "downtown," plunging wholeheartedly into the swirling, dancing, hustling, hair-conking, zoot-suit-wearing, woman-chasing, reefer-smoking fast life of Black Boston. He worked a variety of odd jobs, as shoeshine boy, busboy, soda jerk, factory and shipyard worker, but his heart was in learning the hustler's craft, which was fast becoming his real profession. Soon Boston wasn't big enough for Malcolm. After less than a year, he hit the road to the hustler's capital, New York.

For the next four years, Malcolm was on the move, shuttling between New York, Boston, and Michigan. He worked in a jewelry store, on the railroad, in a defense plant, and he waited tables in Small's Paradise in Harlem, while descending ever deeper into the criminal netherworld. He dealt drugs and pimped; he stuck people up and became a burglar. Except for his ties to his brother Reginald, who lived with him for a time, he seems to have lost all family and moral mooring. On a trip to Boston he steals his aunt's fur coat. In Detroit he robs a friend. He has become a predator without a conscience.

Occasionally flashes of pseudoracial consciousness break through, as in 1942 when he receives his draft notice and goes around Harlem saying that he wants "to fight for the Japanese and kill crackers." This was undoubtedly hype for Malcolm (it got him rejected as "a psychopathic personality"). But back home in Michigan, [Nation of Islam leader] Elijah Muhammad, who would soon help rescue Malcolm from the darkness into which he had fallen, was doing real time in prison for counseling Black men to resist the draft and not fight "our Asiatic brother."

Race politics, however, was actually the farthest thing from Malcolm's mind. He had run afoul of the Harlem numbers runner West Indian Archie and had to return to Boston to avoid being killed. He resumed a relationship with a white woman with whom he had been consorting off and on for years, and together with her friends, they formed an interracial burglary ring, which operated out of an apartment in Harvard Square.

At first they did quite well. But Malcolm eventually got caught trying to recover stolen property from a pawnshop. The white women turned state's evidence, got probation and a suspended sentence, and Malcolm's lover served seven months. Malcolm, on the other hand, received a ten-year sentence—in large part, he believed, because the authorities frowned upon his forbidden relations with the women. (Unbeknownst to Malcolm, he had dodged a more crippling racist bullet when the women, to their credit, resisted police overtures that they accuse Malcolm and his confederates of rape.)

He was sent to Charlestown Prison. The year was 1946, and he was not yet twenty-one years old.

CONVERSION

The [unique circumstances] of Malcolm's transformation in prison, his phoenix-like rise from the ashes of degradation, has added considerably to his legend. Yet in focusing on Malcolm's individual conversion to Islam, we overlook the appeal of Islam to Blacks in general; we overlook the role of human encouragement, which played so significant a part in his self-reappraisal; we overlook the role of his family in recruiting him; and we overlook the damage of racism, which placed Malcolm on the path to nihilism in the first place.

First came the human support he got from his role model in prison, "Bimbi," who was regarded as the smartest convict in the prison and who got respect not with violence or bluster but "with words." It was Bimbi who told Malcolm that he had a mind, if he would only develop it.

It was such a small thing, just a little human encouragement, but it contrasted sharply with his Mason teachers, who had denigrated his achievements and consigned Malcolm, apparently forever, to life as an American outcast (a role he acted out rather well).

Having been awakened to the possibility of new personal growth by Bimbi, Malcolm is approached by his siblings, who want him to join them in their new religion, Islam. Consequently, when Malcolm does join the Nation, he is simply the latest member of his family to do so. Wilfred and Hilda, who helped raise him, were already members, as were Philbert and Reginald, a younger brother with whom he was closest during his hustling days. On one level, then, Malcolm's conversion may be viewed as an act of renewing family ties cut off by personal tragedy or, in Malcolm's case, individual waywardness. It was also a reconnection with those days when their mother read to them from *The Negro World* and their father spoke to them of "the great race work" to be done.

This family history is important because it links Malcolm's individual conversion to the larger social allure of Muhammad's teachings, which impacted on four individuals who had gone their separate ways yet came to common agreement on the nature of racial oppression in America. Seen in this light, the responsibility for Malcolm's conversion is not primarily Malcolm's or Muhammad's or Bimbi's or his siblings'. It is the American denial of human recognition to Blacks that alienated Malcolm—and alienates untold numbers today.

We cannot, however, discount the indisputable importance of Elijah Muhammad's role in Malcolm's conversion, because Muhammad's human sensitivity in reaching out to Malcolm made Malcolm feel a vital part of his new religious-political family. Himself incarcerated by the FBI for sedition, conspiracy, and violation of the draft laws, Muhammad could understand the psyche of a fellow Black convict. He wrote and sent money to Malcolm, who was a perfect stranger. Again were wonders wrought by a little human kindness.

All these forces combined to crack the dam of Malcolm's stunted intellectual development and allow his prodigious natural talent to burst through. Piece by piece, he refined a method of intellectual development that made him one of the great critical thinkers of his or any time.

EDUCATION IN PRISON

The first step was honest self-criticism. Malcolm freely faced up to his faults. His reading comprehension had deteriorated. He practiced writing the alphabet over and over again until his handwriting improved. To cure his ignorance, he embarked on what we might call the "dictionary project," a systematic study from *a* to *z*. The dictionary revived his old love for history and gave him a new interest: philology. But philology is more than a study of words; it is a form of applied logic. And Malcolm was a logician. That's why he loved debating. He liked constructing logical arguments regardless of what side he was on. He used to try to anticipate what the other side might say and prepare responses. Examining both sides of an issue for the purpose of improving one's own argument is intellectual rigor of a high order, and that was a key element of Malcolm's approach: systematic study and reflection.

Then there was history. He had always loved it, but now he had a purpose: to verify the religious-historical claims of the Nation of Islam. So he dove into the books in his typical way: with everything that was in him. He became a *student*, a near-obsessed student, who kept reading long after the prison lights went out and eventually developed astigmatism. But that was Malcolm's way. Whatever he was into, he was into totally.

Malcolm also had genuine intellectual curiosity. As driven as he was to acquire knowledge to expose the crimes of the white West, he would pause sometimes for pure intellectual enjoyment, examining a question that had nothing to do with race, such as the authorship of Shakespeare's plays: "No color was involved there; I just got intrigued over the Shakespearean dilemma."

I think we fail to perceive Malcolm as a true intellectual because we regard as intellectuals those who communicate via the written word and to a certain audience. But Malcolm's [specialty] was the *spoken word*. Moreover, Malcolm tailored his teachings to his audience, whether one of academics, Christians, or folks from the street. He was intellectually flexible, because his first priority was *to communicate* in order to instruct. He spoke to people in the language they understood, because he was a people's intellectual, not an intellectual's intellectual. . . .

It was in prison, then, that Malcolm found his new identity and his calling. Motivated by Bimbi and Muhammad, he became a student and an unofficial minister. He now tutored other inmates, reenacting the path his parents had trod.

EXTENDED FAMILY

Family was important in the life of Malcolm X as it is important in the life of us all. His nuclear family had fought valiantly to preserve itself against the ravages of a jealous racism and an abandoning economy. But when both parents became casualties of this war of racist political economy, and the children's struggle to keep things together could not hold back the tide of disintegration, the Black extended family in the person of Ella Collins intervened to rescue Malcolm at the edge of the engulfing wave. It is only when Malcolm deserts his biological family for the family of the streets that he becomes lost. And he is not "found" again until he reconnects with his family and, through them, connects with the larger racial family embodied in the Nation of Islam and its leader, the Honorable Elijah Muhammad.

That Malcolm loved Elijah Muhammad seems undeniable, for if deeds mirror devotion, no one could possibly have worked harder and therefore loved Elijah Muhammad more than Malcolm. Some have suggested that Malcolm joined the Nation primarily because he saw in Elijah Muhammad a surrogate father. It is true that there are striking similarities in the backgrounds of Earl Little and Elijah Muhammad in the sense that Elijah Muhammad, born in 1897, was, like Earl Little, from a small, racially stratified Georgia town. Like Earl Little, Elijah Muhammad was indifferently educated by what passed for the colored "school system" of those days, reaching only the fourth grade. Like Earl Little, Elijah Muhammad grew up to practice a churchless Baptist ministry alongside the jobs he took to support himself and his young family. And like Earl Little, and many thousands before him, Elijah Muhammad came to despair of ever leading a manly and entitled existence in Klan-run Georgia, so he, too, migrated north in search of the Great Black Dream of a better and a freer life.

Both men reacted to their racial experiences by turning to a religion that espoused a special destiny and purpose for the Black race as distinct from—and in opposition to—the white world. That doctrine was familiar to Malcolm and his siblings because they had absorbed it at their parents' knees. So their subsequent embrace of Elijah Muhammad's Islam seems both psychologically and ideologically natural. . . . It was the dehumanizing Black experience that drew most of the Little family—Wilfred, Hilda, Philbert, and Reginald—into the Nation before Malcolm, and it was that experience, codified into an anti-Christian, anti-white religion and philosophy, which would, in Malcolm's hands, draw in thousands, thousands more.

That was the potential Elijah Muhammad seems to have sensed in his new disciple. Here, at last, was the "son" for whom he had been seeking, the son with the drive and energy and dedication to build a new world in his, Muhammad's, name.

Developing a New Philosophy

Charles G. Hurst Jr.

After listening to the speeches of Nation of Islam leader Elijah Muhammad from within his jail cell, and the endless debating with fellow inmates, Malcolm was ready to create his own philosophy. His new way of thinking, adapted from the teachings of Muhammad, was more than just a vague collection of ideas. What he mapped out during his time in prison would become the guidelines for an entire new college, an organization for the education of black youth. It included how to act, how to think, and how to live free of racism as a strong African American. Charles G. Hurst Jr., writer and educator, was the president of the Malcolm X College, founded by Malcolm X himself. In his book *Passport to Freedom*, published in 1972, he talks about some of the finer points of Malcolm's theories on education.

As [Malcolm's] autobiography points out, life in prison started out to be simply an extension of life in the streets. But he overcame temptations of a prison with more evils than the streets and turned instead to a library for knowledge.

His understandable rage began to settle into a more calculating pattern. Undergirding the struggling rebirth of a soul in torment was a searching need for a spiritual foundation on which a philosophy of life could be constructed. This need was fulfilled shortly after his transfer to Concord prison by his conversion to the Nation of Islam as a follower of the Honorable Elijah Muhammad. He was converted to the orthodox Islam religion before his death.

Despite the persecution by prison officials growing out of their negative attitude toward Muslims, Malcolm persevered both in the study of his new religion and in the quest for knowledge.

Charles G. Hurst Jr., *Passport to Freedom: Education, Humanism, and Malcolm X.* Hamden, CT: The Shoe String Press, Inc., 1972. Copyright © 1972 by The Shoe String Press, Inc. Reproduced by permission.

In addition to his voracious reading in prison, Malcolm began to demonstrate his talent as a leader of men. Instructors who taught at the prison from such prestigious schools as Boston University and Harvard University found him also a formidable opponent in debates on a variety of issues, especially those involving race, racism, exploitation, and injustice. They marveled at the response of other prisoners to Malcolm's exhortations.

During his studies in prison, he became more convinced that endless contradictions existed between what America claimed to be and what it actually was in terms of the treatment accorded its colored and racial minorities. He also concluded that much of the most popular reading material about life in America was based on hypocrisy and outright falsehoods.

He saw with a revealing clarity the difference between segregation and separation. Segregation he described as a condition of life forced upon a people, regulated from the outside. Separation was described as a condition entered into voluntarily by two equals for the good of both.

The penetrating insights of Malcolm, steeped as they were in bitterness, were revealed in the statement that, "All of us who might have probed space, or cured cancer, or built industries were, instead, Black victims of the white man's American social system."

He noted that instead of social contributions that would build humanity, we have a situation where in "every big city ghetto tens of thousands of yesterday's and today's school dropouts are keeping body and soul together by some form of hustling."

Malcolm gave to Black youth a description . . . both apt and appreciated . . . : "Hustler, uneducated, unskilled at anything honorable, but nervy and cunning enough to live by wits, exploiting every prey."

Even while in prison, Malcolm spoke of how Black people were taught to be ashamed of their Blackness, and how their shame led them to become instruments of their own victimization in an almost unbelievable variety of ways. His understanding of how the success image for Black people was always a white ideal, made white listeners writhe then as later when he articulated this understanding in the quiet but firm language of a man who had begun to transcend the destiny originally conceived for him.

Malcolm devised a learning style in prison that was

uniquely suited for an intelligent being deprived of some of the learning tools considered indispensable for success in the usual traditional settings. He virtually devoured a collegiate level dictionary. He would read aloud from his own writing until the page was memorized. The iron-willed discipline is obvious. In prison he developed for himself the equivalent of a college education with a major in humanities. . . .

A PHILOSOPHY DEVELOPS

The guiding precepts of his new life were basic to his continued development as a model for the new kind of Black man he hoped to create in liberating the old kind of Negro from his "slave mentality." He believed that "Heaven and hell were conditions of life endured by people right here on earth; the Black man will never get respect until he learns to respect his woman; freedom, justice, and equality will come about for Black people when they become willing to pay any price necessary to get them; Black people must turn their backs on tobacco, liquor, narcotics, dancing, gambling, movies, lying, stealing, and domestic quarreling."

His enthusiastic dedication was tempered by the knowledge that, "no true leader burdens his following with a greater load than they can carry, and no true leader sets too fast a pace for his followers to keep up."

Malcolm believed that one of the white man's tricks was to keep the Black race divided and fighting each other. "This has traditionally kept Black people from achieving the unity which was the worst need of the Black race in America," he said. His autobiography documents the extent of America's failure in the area of Black-white relations as he saw it: "The Western world's most learned diplomats have failed to solve this grave race problem. Her learned legal experts have failed. Her sociologists have failed. Her civil leaders have failed. Her fraternal leaders have failed.". . .

[Malcolm's] incomprehensibility for white critics was an extension of the lack of information by most whites about Black America's people. "I would hate to be general of an army as badly informed as the American white man has been about the Negro," he said. . . .

He came to see that the condition of Black people was closely related to the plight of other have-nots—the browns, the reds, and even poor whites. His plea became an orchestration on the rights of man.

It was Malcolm who helped Black youth understand that revolution must take place in oneself before he can function

> ### INTEGRATIONISTS AND BLACK NATIONALISTS
> *Malcolm's college, his teachings, and the philosophies he encouraged in the minds of his fellow Muslims were*
> built on a foundation of black separatism. One way to fully understand what his philosophy represented is to look at it as an opposing view to the integrationist theories of Martin Luther King Jr. As thinkers, Malcolm and Martin tended to butt heads, but their ideologies were complementary. Historian James H. Cone helps illuminate the relationship in his book Martin & Malcolm & America.
>
> Integrationists and nationalists complemented each other. Both philosophies were needed if America was going to come to terms with the truth of the black experience. Either philosophy alone was a half-truth and thus a distortion of the black reality in America. Integrationists were *practical.* They advocated what they thought could be achieved at a given time. They knew that justice demanded more. But why demand it if you can't get it? Why demand it if the demand itself blocks the achievement of other desirable and achievable goals? In their struggle for justice, they were careful not to arouse the genocidal instincts inherent in racism. Thus they chose goals and methods which many whites accepted as reasonable and just. The strengths and weaknesses of the integrationist view are reflected in the life and ministry of Martin King.
>
> Nationalists were *desperate.* They spoke for that segment of the African-American community which was hurting the most. Thus, they often did not consider carefully the consequences of their words and actions. The suffering of the black poor was so great that practical or rational philosophies did not arouse their allegiance. They needed a philosophy that could speak to their existence as black people, living in a white society that did not recognize their humanity. They needed a philosophy that empowered them to "respect black" by being prepared to die for it. Overwhelmed by misery, the black poor cried out for relief, for a word or an act that would lift them to another realm of existence where they would be treated as human beings. In place of an American dream, nationalists gave the black poor an African dream. The strengths and the weaknesses of this perspective were reflected in the life and ministry of Malcolm X.
>
> James H. Cone, *Martin & Malcolm & America: A Dream or a Nightmare.* New York: Orbis Books, 1991.

correctly to help others. Youth learned that the truly revolutionary struggle is not based on strategy and tactics alone, but on truth. "It is from truth and truth alone that Black youth must operate. That must be his base; his motive for struggle; his will to survive."

Malcolm was saying essentially that leadership involves responsibility for being a man renewed in spirit, mind, and body. "A man must inspire people and his actions must give a glimpse of what lies ahead. He gives clear direction in work, deed, and in his very being. He is patient, considerate, helpful, compassionate, strong and uncompromising."

Applying all of his powers of analysis to education for the masses, Malcolm concluded that the educational process should unleash a sense of inner power and a recognition of the requirements for group power. Education should empower, not depower.

Selected courses are important only as they are related to reality. The content should flow from the Black experience and

"—from the pragmatic to the theoretical—"

"—from the informal to the formal—"

"—from Black awareness to Black relevant competence—"

"—from teacher sources to student sources—"

"—from group education to self-education—"

"—from the acquisition of basic skills to the application of these skills to real life problems—"

"—from the individual acquisition of ability to the utilization of this new-found ability in the cause of collective Black survival—"

"—from understanding one's membership within the Black nation to the application of one's brain power to the strengthening of that nation's ability to survive—to resist exploitation and to implement its own stated intentions—"

WHAT SHOULD BE DONE

It is the interrelationship of various courses to each other and to real life which makes them relevant. An important key is the student's role in educating himself to learn to love learning for the benefit of his own people. Malcolm believed this and also held the following to be true.

Africanization should pervade the entire educational experience in descriptive, analytical, historical and intellectual terms. The spiritual and human qualities of the experience and the search for a relevant set of values cannot be separated from this process. There is no such thing as a value-free course of curriculum. The Black Experience is *intra*curricular; nothing which affects Black people should be *extra*curricular.

The education of Black people should be controlled and developed and shaped by the Black consensus wherever Black people are being educated. We must stop the massive educational assembly-line production of the "made-in-America Negroes."

A massive educational program should be undertaken at the street corner, doorstep, church pew, and barroom level to stimulate the engagement of a psychological and political confrontation to take over the schools in Black communities.

A national communications network should be established to promote intercity communications—the exchange of information, request for support and as a tool for undertaking nationwide action. A system should be developed to ensure that all federal funds, textbooks, consultancies, etc., that flow into the Black community are controlled by and benefit the local community in educational, economic, and technical terms.

Malcolm's philosophy on education also encompassed the following understandings about the Black community:

> *Black awareness* for the Black community should not be misconstrued as any more than the first step toward returning "home." The nation must be built—psychologically and operationally.

> *Black precipitated crises* serve to heighten awareness to produce the confrontation out of which change becomes possible, and to provide data on which to base the future struggles.

> Think in terms of *the struggle* and not just about winning it. Struggle, in itself, will produce its own victories. Preoccupation with winning may prejudice one against the right to make honest, or even stupid, mistakes. One also learns from mistakes.

> *Demonstrate* to the Black community how the existing system has deliberately succeeded in failing to educate Black students. Use test scores, dropout and unemployment rates, the disproportionate number of Blacks who served in Vietnam, etc. Either one accepts that it has been a deliberate design not to educate Black students or he must accept that Blacks are inferior

in native intelligence. Any man worth a grain of salt knows that Black is beautiful, i.e., that no man is better than any other man just because he is white. If a Black man thinks that he is inferior to anyone, it is only because he has accepted someone else's definition of himself and not really his own deeply concealed knowledge that he is in fact as good as anyone else.

Mobilize and organize the Black community to think, feel, and behave consciously Black. Help brothers and sisters to ask one another how to become Black; *avoid telling* brothers and sisters to be Black. They are already aware of their Blackness; they merely fail to comprehend its positive aspects.

Apply legal strategies as harassment and publicity maneuvers as well as a protection of individual rights. Do not rely excessively on the prospect of winning, but don't reject the victories.

It is not necessary to wait until a *majority* of the Black community is involved. An effective minority may be much more indicative of *what will be*; the majority is usually a reflection of *what used to be.* As you take action, also organize—organizations can flow and flower out of the action, if consciously planned.

Attempt to *cultivate student power* which communicates easily with other segments of the community.

Draw upon the resources of Blacks who work inside the system as sources of information and as advocates within the system.

IDEAS ON SCHOOLING

In addition to the above principles as a renewed basis for racial unity, community control of schools was defined by Malcolm as the power to make and enforce decisions in certain specific areas:

Expenditure of funds—local, state and federal

Hiring and firing of all staff—including training and reprogramming

Site selection and naming of schools

Design and construction of schools—awarding and supervising of contracts

Purchasing power—for books, supplies, equipment, food services, etc.

Setting up of educational policy and programs

Merit pay to staff—increments and salary based on effective performance alone.

The composition of the governing boards of Black-controlled schools, he believed, should involve parents, students, community leaders, and teachers—of the authentically Black variety.

An effort should be made to prevent unions—white or Negro—from negotiating educational policies without the equal participation of Black community representatives. Locally controlled districts of the school might negotiate with the union on parts of the contract; the central agency with equal participation from locally controlled units might negotiate those parts of the contract (excluding salaries) which are appropriate at that level.

Aside from the idea of community control of schools as they currently exist, there is a need to examine parallel systems, operating outside of the public system, because of the system's general bankruptcy as it relates to the Black student. Such a (parallel) system would include private schools, the University of Islam, Afro–American Culture Centers, Liberation Schools, etc. These kinds of schools could serve to convince the Black community of the essential educability of its youth, to experiment with new techniques, to provide local residents with meaningful revolutionary roles, to deepen and expand the supply of effective Black talent, and to increase the possibility that the more frequently overlooked youth are provided with opportunities to increase their inputs to the movement.

Parallel systems should focus on Black history, blackening the curriculum (viewing economic, political, psychological, cultural, historical, sociological, and intellectual aspects as one interrelated body of knowledge), improving basic skills, increasing parental concern and involvement, becoming self-financing, becoming accountable to the Black community, hiring sensitive staff and relating their efforts *relevantly* to the accrediting and credentialing systems.

The curriculum of a parallel system must proceed from the position that the Black child is human and educable, with creative capabilities and potential. It must inculcate a desire to contribute toward Black nationhood and to incorporate an ability to think for one's self. It must be a process of becoming able, as one acquires the basic skills, to learn *how* to make a contribution and *which* contribution he wants to make.

This ideal system, formulating in Malcolm's mind as he

conceived the Organization of Afro–American unity, sees the transmission of knowledge as inseparable from the idea of respect and mutuality: The teacher learns as he teaches; a student teaches his teachers and his classmates as he learns. The student learns as a member of a group, not solely as an individual. Each student is unique but at the same time a member of a group.

Similarly the development of people is not the exclusive domain of the formal school. Learning takes place inside and outside of the classroom. One learns from friends, from parents, and from other "significant" adults in one's life. The community is the classroom. In a bedroom or a playground, one learns as he functions and hopefully has fun as he learns.

With respect to the Black child, he is called upon to incorporate a desire to survive creatively and to acquire the tools of scholarship and to promote them as a component part of his Blackness—his consciousness of it; his skill in determining his own destiny; his desire to sustain and to cultivate his own creativity.

Stated most succinctly, it was Malcolm's position that education must be viewed as a system having definite goals and values. Its prime function was viewed as instilling in students the positive values, ideology, and vision of the system of which they are a part, with a view toward the perpetuation of that particular system. Thus education is seen as far more than merely the teaching of reading, writing, and arithmetic.

Education for Black children and youth as based on these concepts of education and life does not, in consequence, exist in a vacuum. It is an experience in humanism and survival for purposes of supporting the needs, the hopes and the dreams of a society.

Malcolm's Prison Ministry

Louis A. DeCaro Jr.

Through the interviews he conducted and his extensive knowledge of the Malcolm X autobiography, Louis A. DeCaro Jr. took an intense look at the activities of Malcolm while in prison. Of interest to DeCaro was Malcolm's letter writing. During his incarceration, Malcolm sent multiple letters to family, friends, and associates from both his past as a hustler and his future as a member of the Nation. In this passage from *Malcolm and the Cross,* DeCaro examines some of these letters as indicators for the new direction Malcolm's life was about to take, especially his spiritual growth in prison.

"Do you believe in God?" the young inmate asked after accidentally-on-purpose bumping into another inmate in the prison courtyard. "God the father," he continued, "God the son, God the Holy Ghost, and all that crap?" The other inmate, a prisoner-philosopher named Bembry, wasn't offended by the young man because he recognized the sober intent of his question. In a short time the two prisoners, Malcolm Little and John Bembry, became friends—but it was a mentoring friendship, the kind of camaraderie and exchange that fed the intellect and imagination of young Malcolm, helping him to initiate a process of "mental resurrection" which he later attributed to Elijah Muhammad. As he recalled in his autobiography, Malcolm had already been observing Bembry—whom he calls "Bimbi" in his story— and was impressed with the inmate's great store of knowledge. Erudite and seasoned as a student of history, philosophy, and religion, Bembry enjoyed the respect of prisoners and correction officers alike. More interesting, however, is what particularly attracted Malcolm to Bembry: "What made me seek his friendship was when I heard him discuss religion." Even as a young hustler, it seems, religion was never as far from his mind as he would like to have had his readers believe. Not that the teenage Malcolm was seeking religion, but he was thinking about it, if only in rebellion. One Harlem associate even remembered him reading a good deal more than Malcolm admits in *The Autobiography.* Though most of what he was reading was admittedly shallow material, this friend distinctly remembered Malcolm also reading the Bible.

A NEW RELIGIOUS INTEREST

Despite Malcolm's self-portrayal as a rebel and a prison atheist, it appears he carried within him an interest in religious thought throughout his youth. To be sure, as his career in criminal mischief and debauchery deepened, Malcolm's immoral behavior seems to have derailed his religious development. His fascination with lively, sensual urban culture proved to be a far greater force in his adolescence than were the moral teachings of his mother. Still, despite the depravity in which Malcolm became involved, one has a sense that—given his mother's religious orientation and instruction—he had never entirely done away with his personal altar. It is impossible to ascertain what it was about religion that Malcolm found fascinating, but it is safe to suggest that his interest in religion was not simply born from the desperation of his prison cell.

In his years as a teenager running on the streets of Boston, not all of Malcolm's haunts were nightclubs, bars, and pool rooms. In keeping with his mother's example, young Malcolm apparently found at least one church attractive, and for good reason. The Reverend Samuel Laviscount, pastor of St. Mark's Congregational Church (United Church of Christ) in Roxbury, held regular community meetings which drew young people, including some "rough young fellows" like Malcolm Little. It is possible, in fact, that it was Malcolm's involvement that brought such otherwise street-oriented youth to a church—foreshadowing the kind of charismatic influence he would have in drawing people into the Nation of Islam many years later. Malcolm paid attention and participated in questions-and-answers in these forums, and decades afterward Laviscount still remembered teenage Malcolm expressing interest in the condition of blacks living in Scandinavia. The fact that Laviscount later remembered Malcolm is no surprise, since they had established a relationship—the pastor having considered young Malcolm quite nice despite his waywardness. For his part, Malcolm may have been drawn to Laviscount for a number of reasons. Born in Antigua, British West Indies, and schooled at Atlantic Union College (Lancaster, Mass.) and the School of Religion at Howard University, Laviscount manifested two characteristics that Malcolm perhaps found attractive—Caribbean culture and advanced education. Much like his later attraction to the well-read prisoner Bembry, Malcolm was invariably drawn to intellectuals who displayed intensity of thought and learning. Laviscount's West Indian background may have struck a chord of familiarity in Malcolm's life and, of course, there was his abeyant interest in religious matters, which made the learned pastor seem quite appealing. . . .

During his thirty-three-year pastorate at St. Mark's, Laviscount served in many community and pastoral associations, including a seat on the board of directors for the Urban League. His impact on young people was hardly limited to Malcolm—who actually may have proven far more resistant to the Pastor's counsel than other young people, some of whom eventually became leaders in the community. Not that Malcolm did not appreciate Laviscount's advice, but the pull of the urban underworld was still too great. Whatever religious or spiritual advice Laviscount had offered to Malcolm did little good, and there is no way of knowing if he was aware of Malcolm's later incarceration before the young man contacted him. Obviously, throughout his hustler days, Malcolm did not consider an active religious and spiritual life desirable. It was in the shadows of incarceration that a ripening interest in religion occurred, and only after a period of reactionary atheism in which Malcolm delighted in his notorious career of cursing God and mocking faith—an act that caused him to become known around the prison yard as "Satan." However, in the swing back toward religion that occurred in his first conversion, Malcolm personified the very kind of religious experience that his mother had sought to discourage in her children. Investing his faith in Elijah Muhammad, Malcolm became a fundamentalist of sorts, a religious zealot whose canon was not a text, but a man.

When the Reverend Laviscount heard from Malcolm again it was late 1950, and Malcolm had already converted to the

Nation of Islam. At just under two years before his parole (August 1952), Malcolm had become quite advanced in his studies and writing, having already embarked on strategies to enhance and advance the cause of Elijah Muhammad within the Massachusetts prison system. "I've never been one for inaction," Malcolm recalled regarding his first letter-writing endeavors from prison. He says in his autobiography that he made significant efforts to reach his former associates in "the hustling world," though none ever responded, and he assumed his former friends either could not read or found his message too bizarre. But Malcolm apparently wrote to many other people, including the Reverend Laviscount.

In a format that Malcolm would invariably follow in writing letters as a representative of the Nation of Islam, he began with a "Muslim" heading, "In the Name of Allah," which was actually a reference to W.D. Fard ("our Almighty Savior"). Malcolm's conversion had included what he called a "pre-vision" of Fard, a primal experience that seemed to confirm the correspondence he was receiving at the time from Elijah Muhammad. . . .

Malcolm was twenty-five years old when he penned his first prison letter to the Reverend Laviscount, who was sixty-one at the time. The manner of his greeting—the kind generally reserved for peers—was telling. "Dear Brother Samuel," he wrote assuredly, and with the intention of lecturing the pastor, "[w]hen I was a child I behaved like a child, but since becoming a man I have endeavored to put away childish things." This phrase, which Laviscount would certainly have recognized as a reiteration of the words of St. Paul, demonstrated the certainty of the young man's faith in the message of Muhammad. Malcolm continued: "When I was a wild youth, you often gave me some timely advice; now that I have matured I desire to return the favor."

Malcolm may have seemed imperious to Laviscount, whose years of study and experience in the ministry far extended those of the young convert; others had certainly been put off by Malcolm's approach. Earlier in his imprisonment, Malcolm had sought the tutelage of the Watchtower Bible and Tract Society, and a representative consequently initiated a series of visits with him during his stay at the Norfolk Prison Colony. At Norfolk, Malcolm was engaged in an intense and self-motivated period of study prompted by his desire to advance the Nation of Islam. According to J. Prescott

Adams, the Watchtower representative, Malcolm was particularly interested in Jesus; however, the Jehovah's Witness
was apparently perplexed by Malcolm's inclination to compare Jesus with Prophet Muhammad of Islam. Malcolm had
sought out the Watchtower Society for study materials, but
his thoughts on religion were quite out of reach to Adams,
who had undoubtedly hoped to bring the young inmate into
the fold. Instead Adams was privately flustered by his self-
assurance, later concluding that Malcolm was nurturing a
"great ego." Unfortunately, without access to the full correspondence between Malcolm and the Reverend Laviscount,
it is impossible to know if the clergyman drew similar con-
clusions about his young friend, though it is quite certain
that Malcolm would have rejected any counsel that ran contrary to the teachings of Elijah Muhammad. . . .

A MIND CLOUDED BY IGNORANCE

"This sojourn in prison has proved to be a blessing in dis-
guise," Malcolm wrote to Laviscount, "for it provided me
with the Solitude that produced many nights of Meditation."
There are so many things that one never considers, Malcolm
concluded, until "embraced by Solitude, one meets the
FACTS face to face." While the "facts" probably entailed meditations on his intensive course of reading, Malcolm undoubtedly found a great deal of time to reflect on his own life,
too. "I have to admit a sad, shameful fact," Malcolm later
wrote in his autobiography. "I had so loved being around the
white man that in prison I really disliked how Negro convicts
stuck together so much." However, Malcolm concluded, after
Muhammad's teachings had "reversed my attitude toward
my black brothers, in my guilt and shame I began to catch
every chance I could to recruit for Mr. Muhammad."

While Malcolm undoubtedly came to regret the moral debauchery of his hustling days, the sins of his youth, like his
initial attitude about race relations in prison, were not
shameful in and of themselves. His sins, as he came to believe as a Black Muslim, represented a mind clouded by ignorance of self, resulting in a life of compromise and sur-
render to the evil influence of white people. Malcolm
expressed this quite eloquently in his letter to the Reverend
Laviscount:

> The devil[']s strongest weapon is his ability to conventional-
> ize our Thought . . . and rather than exert our own Con-

science, we willfully remain the humble servants of every one else's ideas except our own . . . not even having our own opinions of ourselves or our very own people. . . . [W]e have made ourselves the helpless slaves of the wicked [O]ccidental world.

It seems that Malcolm's prison meditations, encouraged by insightful hours of reading and correspondence with Elijah Muhammad, actually enhanced his shame by the racial associations that now seemed to undergird his former life of sin. In a letter several months before the one to the Reverend Laviscount, Malcolm wrote to his brother Philbert: "Brother, you don't really know the devil until you've lived with him. He is one thing that I'm an expert on! I have lived and participated with him in *every* phase of his life!" Malcolm was undoubtedly thorough in his understanding—perhaps more than any other African American leader of his era, the young man who would become famous for heaping contempt upon "white devils" was intimately acquainted with the ways of white folks. From the church and the classroom to the nightclub and the brothel, Malcolm's troubled sojourn had allowed him to see the full spectrum of white racist attitude and behavior. "I can talk much trash about the devil, convincingly," Malcolm also wrote to his brother Philbert. In another letter, written to Philbert's new wife, Malcolm likewise declared: "The many contacts I have had with the devil made it easy for me to recognize him as the devil. I find that the only reason many Originals [*African Americans*] are hesitant to accept the Truth is that their association with the devil has been superficial and they don't know him well enough to *see* his true character.". . .

RECRUITING

In the first years, especially within prison, Malcolm had done a significant amount of recruiting and teaching. Even his most cynical biographer notes that Malcolm's work at Norfolk was "no small achievement," since he had recruited more than a dozen of the eighty blacks incarcerated there. Malcolm's drive to fish for converts was characteristically strong, leaving no stone unturned in his quest for recruitment in the black community. Initially, Malcolm's methods were basic, such as working the fringes of other speakers' audiences in the streets, holding public rallies, waiting to speak to Christians exiting from their churches on Sunday, and distributing printed materials. As Malcolm developed new temples in various cities, of course, he had additional bases from which to reach out to the black population. Along with his growing familiarity with the black community in differing cities across the country, Malcolm developed a keen and sometimes opportunistic use of the black press, especially the major black publications of the day. In some cases it seems he fed exciting articles about Muhammad and himself to papers like the *New York Amsterdam News* and the *Pittsburgh Courier*, lending the impression that the Black Muslims were far more sophisticated and successful than they were in actuality. With national notoriety, Malcolm mastered the art of negative publicity, capitalizing on appearances on antagonistic talk show forums and other unsympathetic radio and television broadcasts, to give the Nation of Islam air play that would otherwise have been unattainable by Elijah Muhammad.

Early in his public ministry, however, Malcolm zealously advanced Elijah Muhammad while the private, philosophical aspects of his prison reflections on God and redemption seem to have receded. There was perhaps a pragmatic side to this development, since Malcolm recognized that other Black Muslim evangelists were probably less capable at explaining and defending the theology of the Nation of Islam. "Never try and teach them too much on the personal [identity] of ALLAH," Malcolm urged his brother Philbert in 1954, "but let your every word and effort be pointing toward the Messenger, letting all your followers know that ELIJAH THE PROPHET is in the land. Lead them toward Him, and HE will lead them toward ALLAH. You bear witness to the one [whom] YOU know, and HE bears witness to the one whom HE KNOWS." However, it is also the case that Malcolm truly came to believe that Muhammad had a unique and authoritative insight into the nature of the divine by revelation. Rather than speak of Fard, whom he believed he had seen in a prison pre-vision, Malcolm emphasized Muhammad. To Malcolm, Elijah Muhammad was "the only Muslim in North America qualified to represent ALLAH (that is, His IDENTITY)," while his ministers would only "mess it up" and "drive the people away." "So let them know that ELIJAH is in the land," Malcolm concluded, "lead them to him, and you will see the people come to you in droves. That is what is making the East Coast remain AFLAME. ELIJAH THE

PROPHET Is the KEY." Of course, Malcolm's sincere faith and upper-case letters notwithstanding, it was not Muhammad who had set the East Coast aflame, but his own zeal. . . .

PRISON MINISTRY

If any aspect of Malcolm's pioneering work among the "grass roots" has been overlooked . . . it is his prison ministry. The importance of his prison ministry is twofold, for it not only represents the new dynamic of Islam (cultic and, eventually, traditional forms) as a vital religious presence in the prison system, but also the requisite corollary to Malcolm's activism against the racism of urban policemen. One inmate, Mahmud Ramza (whose Black Muslim name was Walter 5X), recalls that it was Malcolm who first won the legal privilege to administer religious rites to him while he was incarcerated in New York State's Green Haven Correction Facility in the late 1950s. Through Malcolm's tutelage, Ramza became a significant promoter of "Islam" in the prison system and later an active member of the Nation of Islam. Malcolm's impact on prisoners went far beyond Ramza's case, according to Justice Jawn Sandifer, who served as chairman of the Legal Redress Committee for the New York State Conference of the National Association for the Advancement of Colored People (NAACP). In the 1950s and early 1960s, Sandifer and another NAACP lawyer, Edward Jacko, had their law office in Harlem on 125th Street and came to know Malcolm, serving as counsel for the Nation of Islam in a number of legal suits. Sandifer, who became a New York State Justice in 1964, remembers Malcolm "recruiting people who had previously had some encounter with the law," including drug addicts and hardened criminals, and that he was particularly interested in prisoners. At first, Malcolm was prevented from ministering in the New York State prison system because he was an ex-offender and because his credentials as a "Muslim" minister were not recognized. In that era, Sandifer says, only Protestantism, Roman Catholicism, and Judaism were recognized and represented in the system. "We had to find a way of getting Malcolm recognized as a minister," Sandifer recalls. Despite the fact that the two NAACP attorneys were authorized to move throughout the state prison system, they could not bring Malcolm inside with them. After a number of trips were made to the state capital of Albany in order for Malcolm and the lawyers to appeal to officials, Sandifer began to realize that

> the bottom line was that they were afraid of Malcolm X be-
> cause they didn't know what his real intentions were. . . .
> [B]ased upon their background checks on Malcolm and who
> he was, they were afraid of what Malcolm might potentially
> do if he were able to convert large numbers of these people
> inside the prison walls.

Sandifer says that Malcolm eventually won the right to do
pastoral visitations only because his positive influence on
ex-offenders was undeniably successful. "Malcolm worked
magic," Sandifer recalls. "I can't give you the answer as to
what it was, how one man could take people with criminal
backgrounds—practically every one of them were people
that came out of those prisons." Though Malcolm was quick
to credit Elijah Muhammad with the remarkable rehabilita-
tion of so many ex-offenders, Sandifer recognized the real
influence. "How could a man like Malcolm come into the
prisons, communicate with them, and after they were out,
bring them down to [Temple No. 7 in Harlem]? Malcolm
gave them dignity, he made them productive . . . the same
men that came out of these prisons."

Given Malcolm's determination to use *The Autobiography*
to glorify Elijah Muhammad, it is no surprise that his narra-
tive overlooks his strenuous determination to reach incarcerated men. While Muhammad had interest in prisoners,
Malcolm single-handedly cut a path into the prison system
on behalf of "Islam," a path that has since become well traveled by Black Muslims and traditional Muslims alike. Malcolm was never allowed to speak to large numbers of prisoners, but he worked out an arrangement whereby he
received referrals from Sandifer and Jacko, allowing him to
travel throughout the state prison system, even visiting inmates at maximum-security facilities like Attica. According
to Sandifer, Malcolm particularly focused on prisoners who
made no religious self-identification at the time of their entrance interviews. He may have chosen this approach to
avoid being perceived as a threat to Christian chaplains, but
it may also reflect his hope of reaching men who were wide
open to the message of "Islam."

Malcolm's early and often overlooked work in prison
ministry and justice issues demonstrates his determination
to work with integrationist-oriented groups like the NAACP
long before his brief and notable last year of independent ac-

tivism. Furthermore, his prison ministry shows that Malcolm's interest in justice continued to grow as an *expression of his religious activism,* not in tension with it. . . .

[And finally, the fact] that Malcolm's prison outreach and quest for justice were so unusual in the urban North is as much a tribute to his religious commitment to the downtrodden as it is a sad commentary on the introversion of many black Christian churches.

Support from His Family

Rodnell P. Collins

Prison inmates and stories about Elijah Muhammad and the Nation were not Malcolm's only companions during his incarceration. His family stuck close to him throughout; eventually they were even indirectly responsible for getting him out of jail early. Rodnell P. Collins, a nephew of Malcolm X, gives us a first-hand account of how the Little family manipulated the prison system for Malcolm. They managed not only to get Malcolm released, but helped motivate Malcolm in the direction of the Nation of Islam.

When Uncle Malcolm was sentenced to serve ten years in prison, in February 1946, Ma and Uncle Reginald, one of his younger brothers, were in the courtroom. "I was still angry with him," she said, "for the situation he had gotten himself into. The first time he got arrested, in March 1945, I bailed him out by using our house as collateral. This time I refused to bail him out because of his attitude. In fact, I told him that since he refused to listen to me and other family members, maybe you want the white man to teach you."

Prison Visits

Despite her frustration and anger, Ma was Malcolm's first visitor after he was sent to prison. Of it he wrote: "l remember seeing her catch herself, then try to smile at me, now in the faded dungarees stenciled with my number. Neither of us could find much to say, until I wished she hadn't come at all. . . ."

Ma's recollections were slightly different. "It was not a very pleasant visit. Malcolm was as jive-talking, cocky, and unrepentant as ever. He showed no remorse or concern about family anxiety and seemed to believe that his only problem was being caught, that the next time he would be a smarter hustler. When I left after that visit, I was as upset as I had ever been with him."

Ma wasn't the only one upset with Uncle Malcolm's attitude and actions, which included getting high on drugs bought from prison guards. His siblings in Lansing were equally concerned and upset. They wrote him letters of support and encouragement daily and were disturbed by his seemingly cavalier attitude toward the situation he was in. When Aunt Hilda came to stay with us in Boston, she went to see Uncle Malcolm in prison. After a couple of visits, she was so disgusted with his attitude that during her next trip to Boston, she refused to see him. When he heard about that, Malcolm wrote, in a letter to Ma, "It really hurt to hear that Hilda had gone all the way back to Detroit before she came to see me. . . ." He seemed to have no clue that his attitude was the problem.

A four-page letter he wrote to Ma, dated September 10, 1946, shows just how insensitive he was during his first year or so in prison. It included the following: "The person that you said called me is a very good friend of mine. He's only worth some fourteen million dollars. If you read the society pages you'd know who he is. He knows where I am now because I've written and told him, but I didn't say what for. He may call and ask you. Whatever answer you give him will have to do with my entire future but I still depend on you. . . ."

Ma said the friend never called again, but "I was outraged that Malcolm had given my number to such a person and actually expected me to be a kind of courier between them. I assumed that that 'friend' was one of those decadent whites whom he had been hustling."

The one sensitive note he struck in that same letter was about photographs she had sent to him. "I want to thank you for sending me the pictures. . . . They offer more consolation than anything else, Ella. They keep my mind diverted from my troubles, so please don't stop sending them. I have received what money you've left for me always. I just don't like to mention it. Maybe you can understand; I can't. All I know is when I mention it I feel ashamed. . . ." Maybe Uncle did feel ashamed for he wrote in his autobiography: "With some money sent by Ella, I was finally able to buy stuff for better highs from guards in the prison. . . ."

When Ma visited Uncle Malcolm in prison, she often took

me along. I remember his putting me on his knee while they talked. Sometimes he would tell me stories, which became parables as I got older. I thought of Uncle Malcolm as a big brother who gave me a small table and chair that he made in the prison workshop. He also made musical jewelry boxes, which he gave to a few family members. At least one of them, given to his cousin, Clara Little, is still in existence, owned by her son, John Walker Jr.

FAMILY SUPPORT

Ma said it seemingly didn't occur to Uncle Malcolm that while his brothers and sisters loved him dearly, they were not prepared to support his irresponsible behavior and attitude. She was especially outraged by his treatment of Aunt Sas and Aunt Gracie. Uncle Malcolm loved his two elderly aunts, but he resented their constantly pushing Christianity on him. . . .

Though Ma shared Uncle Malcolm's reservations about Aunt Sas and Aunt Gracie's Christianity, she was very upset by his request that she never again bring them to visit him. "I reminded him how much they loved him, how to them he was a connection to their dead brother, how sincerely concerned they were about his future. They expressed fear to me that 'the devil' was trying to take control of their beloved nephew." Aunt Sas and Aunt Gracie weren't too far off target with that observation. Uncle Malcolm, in a chapter called "Satan," said his cellmates called him "Satan" because of his antireligious attitude.

Because of that attitude and because I suffered from asthma as a child, Ma said she seldom visited Uncle Malcolm during his first year in prison. That upset him; despite what he had done to himself and his family . . . he fully expected Ma to back him all the way without questions or doubts, as she had done so often in the past. "I decided to be cool until he came to his senses," Ma said. "I never believed for a moment that my brother was a confirmed criminal."

Neither did his brothers and sisters and other family members. Despite his nonchalant attitude, his siblings sent him a steady supply of letters of encouragement. Other family members and friends visited as often as possible. His most frequent family visitors during that time were his brother Reginald and his sister Mary. Family and friends were shocked to discover that he could get high smoking marijuana while locked up. This doesn't shock us [today], but in the 1940s it was news to most everyone that prisoners had relatively easy access to drugs. "We were concerned but didn't know what to do about it, since Malcolm seemed determined to smoke as much reefer as he could get his hands on," Ma noted.

It was the reefer smoking that especially angered Aunt Hilda and caused her to stop visiting him on trips to Boston. But she, Ma, and all the others continued writing, convinced that Uncle Malcolm would come around. They knew their brother, knew that his bark was greater than his bite. The observation made by his brother Philbert in the book *Malcolm X: Make It Plain* probably best sums up his siblings' feelings about their then misguided brother.

> He didn't have the temerity, I suppose you'd call it, to be bad. Malcolm was good. Everybody who knew Malcolm would tell you he was a good man. And this is before he came into Islam. He was not vulgar. And he wasn't disrespectful of your rights. He was a braggadocio. He would brag about what he had done and this and that, but it hadn't been that bad. He just knew how to tell it so it sounded as though he was a gang leader. But he didn't have no gang. . . . I learned that he was a hell-raiser (initially) in prison because he was trying to organize people as though he was going to break out and all that kind of stuff. . . .

PAST LOVES

Two of Uncle Malcolm's most frequent visitors during his early prison years were Evelyn, to whom he had once been engaged, and Jackie Massey, who had every intention of marrying him. Ma cared deeply for Evelyn and was very angry when Malcolm broke their engagement. Despite the broken engagement, she urged Evelyn to hang in there until Malcolm saw the light. It was only a few years ago that I found out why Malcolm broke the engagement. He never talked about it to anyone as far as I know, not even to Ma. But Evelyn told her best friend since childhood, Beverly Wilson, who is now one of my close friends, and Beverly told me. Uncle Malcolm was afraid that both of them had people suffering from mental illness in their families. He had heard unconfirmed rumors of mental illness in Evelyn's family, and he had also been convinced by public officials in Michigan that his mother was afflicted with mental illness. He and Evelyn might pass such traits on to their children, so it was impossible for them to marry. Ma was very upset when she later heard about Uncle Malcolm's fears. "It's a tragedy that he believed that," she said. "As far as I know, and I've known Evelyn's family for many, many years, there was no mental illness in her family, at least not the kind that is passed on by genes. As for Malcolm's mother, I still believe that all she suffered was a nervous breakdown brought on by the pressures of her husband's violent death at the hands of white supremacists and of having to deal with the hostility and indifference shown by the state of Michigan and many blacks in Lansing towards her and her children. I don't think she was mentally ill. She thought that if she went along with the state's position, they would see that her children were taken care of." The idea that Uncle Malcolm broke his engagement with Evelyn because he had been misled about mental illness in their families caused Ma great pain. . . .

Uncle Malcolm's second frequent female visitor was Jackie Massey, who lived across the street from us on Dale Street. Ma, like most women in the neighborhood, regarded Miss Massey as a "common street woman" and disliked her as intensely as she liked Evelyn. A few years ago Dad told me that Uncle Malcolm revealed to him that Miss Massey had seduced him not too long after he came to Boston. Dad said he came home early one day from work and found Uncle Malcolm and Miss Massey indulging in some serious carrying on. He never told Ma about this, fearing that she might explode. Ma said, "I didn't know all the details, but I was well aware of how much havoc an older, experienced, predatory woman could wreak on a teenaged, adventurous, highly impressionable wannabe city slicker like Malcolm was at that time."

Besides, she had heard other interesting things about Miss Massey from Uncle Malcolm himself. According to Ma, during her prison visits, Malcolm, for the first time, filled her in on some aspects of his street life in Boston and Harlem, including a business deal he and Malcolm Jarvis had with an elderly, wealthy white millionaire named Paul Lennon, who would pay them to rub powder over his body. He was the wealthy man Uncle Malcolm referred to in a previously mentioned letter to Ma. Lennon's current powderer was Frank Cooper, who had sometimes visited him with Uncle Malcolm and Jarvis. Since Cooper was ostensibly Miss Massey's lover, Ma wondered what was the deal with her and Malcolm.

When Malcolm told Ma that he was now trying to convert Jackie Massey to Islam, she said, "That may be your goal, but hers is to marry you. I can't support such action."

If Ma had had her way, Miss Massey wouldn't have been allowed to visit Uncle Malcolm at all. But she didn't, and Miss Massey, loaded down with the kind of home-cooked food she knew Uncle Malcolm loved, visited him probably more than anyone else. She rode up to Norfolk Prison Colony with members of Jarvis's family, which solidified Ma's hostility toward a man she considered a bad influence on her brother. Ma was so concerned about what she scathingly referred to as "the Jackie Massey mess" that she told Malcolm, "I'd rather see you stay in jail than get out and be with Jackie Massey." Her concerns were such that she refused to sponsor his parole. Uncle Wilfred and Aunt Ruth, his wife, became his sponsors. . . .

THE FAMILY JOINS THE NATION

Not too long after Malcolm's imprisonment, his brother Wilfred joined the Nation of Islam. "I came into the Muslim movement in 1947," Wilfred said, "and started bringing my brothers and sisters in. We already had been indoctrinated with Marcus Garvey's philosophy [of black separatism], so that was just a good place for us. They didn't have to convince us we were black and should be proud or anything like that. We had learned that from our Garveyite parents." Soon Reginald, Philbert, Hilda, and Wesley joined their older brother in the Nation of Islam. The Little siblings didn't just join the Nation; they became some of its most dedicated members and effective proselytizers, especially Wilfred. With the support of his siblings and his wife, Ruth, he set up temples in Michigan, Ohio, and Indiana. Wilfred also became head of Temple One in Detroit. . . .

Wilfred, Ma said, was the kind of organizer that Malcolm would later become when he joined the Nation. "My brothers put their time, skill, money, and tenacity to work building up the Nation of Islam. They would use their own money, if necessary, to carry out its objectives. If it hadn't been for them, the Nation of Islam wouldn't have grown so fast and so large. They really believed that what they were doing was carrying out the legacy left them by their parents.". . .

Slowly, Uncle Malcolm began to respond positively to the urgings of his brothers and sisters. Ma said that initially she was not sure what the Nation of Islam could do for Uncle Malcolm, but "I trusted the judgment of Wilfred, Hilda, and Philbert. If they believed that the organization could rescue our brother from those people and those influences that had encouraged him to run the streets of Boston and Harlem, I was prepared to strongly support their efforts. After they began working on him, I could see a real change in his attitude. There was also a practical aspect to Malcolm's new attitude. He wanted to be transferred to the Norfolk Prison Colony and began to understand that unfocused belligerence resulting from a misguided, ineffective street attitude was not the best way to secure a transfer and possible parole.". . .

GETTING OUT

Malcolm, who had already been transferred from Charlestown prison to Concord, knew that one had to be a model prisoner to be considered for transfer to Norfolk. He also knew, from rumors circulating among the inmates, that money and connections were also needed to facilitate such a transfer. Once he found out about Norfolk, and encouraged by his brothers and sisters, Malcolm's drive and go-get-it attitude, along with his discipline, came into play. He would take care of the model-prisoner requirement; he depended on Ma for the money and connection requirements. Now that he was getting serious about his future, Ma was ready to assist in any way she could. She arranged the transfer with the help of a local black political operative and white judge, both of whom she knew. Of course, there were some funds involved. There was then, and probably is now, such a man in practically every black community in this country. He was the person whom white politicians, police, and public officials choose to use as their "man" in black communities. Thus, he was the person to whom many black people turned when in need of a favor from downtown. What that person provided those white folks for doing the favor was probably different in every city. In Boston's Lower Roxbury section he owned a popular and illegal after-hours club which could only stay open if one had a "you scratch my back, I scratch yours" arrangement with white politicians, police, and other public officials. It was 1951, Aunt Hilda told Ma: "We heard from Malcolm. He was denied parole for another year and Malcolm Jarvis got his. I guess you know that by now I think they are trying to break him down."

"Hilda was right on target," Ma said. "They were trying to break Malcolm down, to goad him into doing something rash and stupid. But the Malcolm they were dealing with in 1951 and 1952 was quite different from the hedonistic, misguided, street-influenced Malcolm they had dealt with in 1946. Due to the encouragement and support of his brothers and sisters and his own focused direction, he was not going to fall into their trap. Once Malcolm decided on a goal, he went for it. And he wanted to get out of prison so he could join his brothers and sisters in their efforts to carry on the legacy of their parents."

The strategy developed by the Little brothers and sisters paid off, leading to Malcolm's parole in August 1952. Wilfred signed his parole-sponsorship papers and procured from his employer a promise to hire Malcolm for a permanent job upon his release from prison. That meant he had to relocate to Detroit. "We all agreed that Boston would not be the best place for him," Ma said, "because the police there would use any excuse to constantly harass him. They knew him as an undisciplined, jive-talking, conk-haired, zoot-suit-wearing petty criminal and, we were sure, wouldn't accept the fact that he had become a disciplined, self-respecting, focused black man who had diligently used his time in prison to vastly expand his knowledge of history and current affairs. I am convinced they would much prefer to deal with the former Malcolm Little rather than with the person he had become."

CHAPTER 3

THE NATION
OF ISLAM

PEOPLE
WHO MADE
HISTORY

MALCOLM X

Malcolm's Leadership

William H. Banks Jr.

The following article is from the book The Black
Muslims. *It gives a relatively nonjudgmental summary of the world inside the Nation of Islam, with a
special focus on the rise of Malcolm from a new recruit fresh out of prison to a spot at the very top of
the organization. As a historian, William H. Banks Jr.
takes us through the travails of Malcolm's leadership
in the Nation with a much less biased perspective
than other writers who lived through those times.*

Malcolm's brothers Philbert and Reginald and his sister
Hilda had been writing to him for some time about their
conversion to what they called the "natural religion for the
black man," the Nation of Islam. Their brother had always
responded to their letters with crude, sarcastic insults. But
by the time Malcolm was transferred to Norfolk Prison in
Massachusetts in 1948, he was ready to listen. A letter from
Reginald ended with a strange proposition. "Don't eat any
pork, and don't smoke any more cigarettes. I'll show you
how to get out of prison."

Intrigued by his brother's words, Malcolm followed his instructions and waited for the solution to this riddle. As time
went on, Reginald taught him more and more about the Nation of Islam, and Malcolm was deeply moved by the teachings of Elijah Muhammad. "You don't even know who you
are," Reginald wrote. "[T]he white devil has hidden it from
you, that you are a race of people of ancient civilizations, and
riches in gold and kings. . . . You have been cut off by the
devil white man from all true knowledge of your own kind."

For Malcolm, who had had little direction in his life, these
words rang true. Most of the hardship he had experienced
could be attributed to whites, and he had read much about
the horrors of slavery in the Americas and about European
colonialism in Africa. But what captivated him most was the

idea of a black cultural history, one whose roots were established in ancient Africa, long before the European slave trade. He was not the isolated misfit he had believed himself to be, but part of a proud race with a rich heritage going back thousands of years.

The Nation gave Malcolm the hammer with which to pound out his rage. He began studying Muhammad's teachings with a zeal that would endure for many years, and with his new beliefs came a renewed determination to improve his mind. His regimen of self-improvement was in keeping with the Nation's credo of discipline: mental, spiritual, and moral. . . .

THE NEW RECRUIT

In August 1952, Malcolm X's exemplary behavior earned him an early release from prison, and he headed immediately for his brother Wilfred's home in Detroit. There he became active in the operation of the Nation's Temple Number One, established by [Wallace] Fard and Muhammad nearly 20 years earlier. Soon after, he went to Chicago to meet Muhammad and hear him preach. The new recruit was nearly overwhelmed with awe for the man who was said to be the Messenger of Allah. Muhammad was likewise struck by the enthusiasm of this bright young apostle.

One day, Malcolm summoned the nerve to bring to Muhammad's attention the dwindling number of followers attending Temple Number One in Detroit. Muhammad agreed that it was a problem and urged Malcolm X to recruit new members. "Go after the young people," he said. "Once you get them, the older ones will follow through shame."

In recruiting expeditions known to Black Muslims as "fishing," Malcolm X began speaking to people in Detroit's bars and poolrooms and on street corners. Having been an outcast and a criminal himself, Malcolm's keen awareness of their experiences helped him find the precise words to persuade them to reform. Prison inmates, who would hear about the Nation in much the same way as Malcolm had, were particularly attracted to its message and converted in droves. After only a few months, Malcolm managed to triple the membership of Temple Number One, and he would win thousands more converts in the years to come. . . .

During the 1950s, the Nation expanded at a tremendous pace. The organization began to hold national meetings. Declaring February 26—Fard's birthday—"Savior's Day," the Nation drew thousands of members to Chicago for the annual celebration. It also staged huge rallies, called Living Fountain assemblies, in many cities. By the end of the decade, the movement had 50 temples in operation. And although the Nation was reluctant to disclose its membership, estimates in the late 1950s and early 1960s showed at least 50,000 believers, of whom 10 to 30 percent were registered followers; many thousands more who were not affiliated with the movement were sympathizers with the Nation's tenets. Much of this growth was attributed to the zealous labor of Malcolm X.

As the Nation of Islam flourished, it became a more established institution than the transitory fringe group many critics had thought it to be. The small-business efforts of the Black Muslims, which had begun with Muhammad's grocery, bakery, and restaurant, now included grocery stores, apartment buildings, factories, farms, cleaning establishments, restaurants, bakeries, and repair-service shops. At one point during the 1950s, the combined wealth of Black Muslim enterprises was estimated at $10 million. By 1960, the Nation owned a half million dollars' worth of real estate in the Chicago area alone. In 1961 the Nation began publishing its own newspaper, *Muhammad Speaks*, a weekly periodical sold by Black Muslim members who received a fraction of the profits. The paper—founded by Malcolm X, who was later appointed editor—eventually became the largest black publication in the country, with a circulation of a half million. . . .

RISING IN THE RANKS

Having gained a larger audience, Malcolm escalated his verbal attacks on "the white devil." The spotlight on the Nation of Islam intensified in 1959 when an African-American journalist, Louis Lomax, acquired Muhammad's consent to make a television documentary on the Black Muslims.

Members of the Nation were pleased that their organization had merited national media coverage. They presumed that such widespread publicity would help to promote the Nation of Islam's teachings and attract new followers.

But they soon learned otherwise. Entitled "The Hate that Hate Produced," the television program, narrated by journalist Mike Wallace, vividly depicted the deep resentment the

Black Muslims and their supporters felt for white society, and presented graphic evidence that a storm of rebellion was gathering in the black ghettos of America. Most white Americans were shocked and horrified to learn of the intense bitterness African Americans felt toward them; they were appalled to hear that blacks thought them the embodiment of evil. The scorching words of Malcolm X, which peppered the documentary, filled them with fear, guilt, and distaste.

The Nation of Islam began drawing the country's attention at a time when racial discrimination was one of the most hotly debated issues in America. During the 1950s, while Malcolm X was delivering his fiery message of black separatism to urban ghetto dwellers in the North, a young minister named Martin Luther King, Jr., was leading a boycott of segregated bus services in Montgomery, Alabama. All over the South, civil rights organizations, such as the Southern Christian Leadership Conference (SCLC) and the Congress on Racial Equality (CORE), were challenging racial segregation in public schools and theaters, in restaurants and rest rooms, on trains and buses. Although the nonviolent protest marches led by King and his colleagues often met with brutal retaliation from white policemen and white supremacist organizations, members of the civil rights movement were beginning to feel hope that they could erode racial discrimination in the South. . . .

Civil rights activists like King won much praise for their courageous fight for racial integration—but not from Malcolm X. He openly scorned their goals and tactics. "You can sit down next to white folks—on the toilet," he remarked, belittling recent rulings outlawing segregated rest rooms. He had nothing but contempt for would-be white allies and had no use for African Americans who believed in an integrated society. He could not abide the idea of imploring whites to provide basic human rights for those who should already have them. Nor did he believe whites would voluntarily accord blacks these rights.

Instead, Elijah Muhammad and Malcolm X began speaking of a separate state for blacks within the United States, as Wallace Fard had done years earlier. "The Negro must think in terms of bettering himself, and this he can only do by thinking in terms of his own black civilization," Muhammad told a *New York Times* reporter in 1963. When slavery was legally abolished in 1865, the government had promised every freed slave 40 acres of land and a mule as compensation for the injustices each had suffered. A century later, African Americans still had not been vindicated. Muhammad was specific in his demands for restitution: "We believe that our former slave-masters are obligated to maintain and supply our needs in this separate territory for the next 20 to 25 years—until we are able to produce and supply our own needs." And Malcolm X, opposing King's peaceful protest methods and vision of a fully integrated and peaceful society, called on African Americans to fight for their constitutional rights and defend themselves without hesitation when attacked—bullet for bullet, if necessary. . . .

CHALLENGES

Once the general public became aware, through media coverage, of the Nation's white-man-as-devil teachings, members of the organization found it increasingly difficult to rent and purchase church halls and other accommodations to hold meetings and establish new temples. In July of 1957, Roy Wilkins, the executive secretary for the NAACP, issued an official statement blasting Muhammad's radical stance: "For years the NAACP has been opposed to white extremists for preaching hatred of Negro people, and we are equally opposed to Negro extremists preaching against white people simply for the sake of whiteness."

Nevertheless, Black Muslims remained adamantly opposed to desegregation and were insulted by the Christian philosophy of turning the other cheek. Such attitudes, the Nation believed, encouraged self-hate, the greatest crime possible against oneself and one's own kind. Moreover, living in an integrated society with the ancestors of slave owners was an abomination to Black Muslims. The white man was doomed—his 6,000 years of dominion were at an end—and any black man who integrated with the corrupt white world would be destroyed along with it. The solution, said Black Muslims, was complete separation of blacks from whites. . . .

Other challenges awaited the Black Muslims. Prison authorities had begun prohibiting incarcerated members of the Nation from practicing their religion. After some of the inmates protested, the Nation filed suits, and two cases were heard by the U.S. Supreme Court. In one case, Black Muslim inmates in California claimed a violation of the Fourteenth Amendment, which guarantees freedom of religion. In the other case, Black Muslims in a New York prison accused authorities of violating the Civil Rights Act of 1871, which maintains that all citizens may practice their chosen religion without government interference. In both cases, the Supreme Court ruled that it was "constitutionally permissible" to deny Black Muslims the right to practice their religion because it threatened national security.

Soon after these decisions, the FBI tightened its surveillance of the Nation, which it had begun in 1941. Government officials were especially concerned with the Fruit of Islam, the Nation's highly trained military corps. Believing that Muhammad was raising his own army, the federal agents wiretapped members' telephones and placed some of them under surveillance.

By this time, Muhammad's health had begun to deteriorate. Malcolm X had already captured America's attention with the airing of Mike Wallace's 1959 television documentary. Always smartly dressed, stately, and with a gift for blazing rhetoric, Malcolm X was an imposing figure. Journalists and television crews sought him out whenever they needed a statement by the Black Muslims. Although Malcolm X— properly—always advised the media to consult Muhammad directly, Muhammad was a small, reserved, soft-spoken man who lacked the commanding, telegenic presence of his disciple. The media continued to spotlight Malcolm X.

In 1962, Malcolm X became the official spokesperson of the Nation of Islam when Muhammad appointed him national minister of the movement. Although Muhammad retained ultimate control over the Nation, Malcolm X was now formally recognized not only as acting head of the movement but as heir apparent to Elijah.

Malcolm Carries the Message of the Black Muslims

Louis E. Lomax

As an African American who lived through the heyday of the Nation of Islam's influence on the black community, Louis E. Lomax wrote extensively on the subject. His writings, advertised as informative and neutral research, often swayed toward a very pro-Nation attitude and tone. Lomax conducted interviews with Nation members and spent time listening to their speeches. In an introduction to his 1963 book, Lomax claims to "differ with them on many issues," but admits that "it is encouraging . . . that a group like the Black Muslims not only lives among us but that it can be investigated and studied." In the following selection, Lomax talks in glowing terms about the Nation's present and future. Following his own writings is an interview with Malcolm X, in which Lomax sets up a series of easily answered questions designed to get the word out about the Nation's philosophy.

The ultimate comment upon racialism in this republic is that the all-black Nation of Islam—a Chicago-based theocracy whose citizens are known as the Black Muslims—is one of the few religions ever produced by the American experience. Incensed liberals, Negro and white, will deny my assertion that the Black Muslims are a religious body, but the issue, both legally and theologically, has been settled: Courts in several states have ruled that the followers of The Honorable Elijah Muhammad are, indeed, adherents to a religious faith—as such, Black Muslim prison inmates have the right to hold services of worship as do other convicts. And no one who understands theologian Paul Tillich's argu-

ment that religion is nothing more than one's ultimate concern can doubt that the teachings of number-two Black Muslim leader, Malcolm X, constitute a religion.

MALCOLM'S CALL

Malcolm X is the St. Paul of the Black Muslim movement.
Not only was he knocked to the ground by the bright light of
truth while on an evil journey, but he also rose from the dust
stunned, with a new name and a burning zeal to travel in the
opposite direction and carry America's twenty million Negroes with him.

"This is the day of warning," Malcolm shouts to the Negro, "the hour during which prophecy is being fulfilled before your very eyes. The white man is doomed! Don't integrate *with* him, separate *from* him! Come ye out from among
the white devils and be ye separate."

Nobody knows just how many Negroes have said "yes" to
Malcolm X's call. Estimates of the Black Muslim membership vary from a quarter of a million down to fifty thousand.
Available evidence indicates that about one hundred thousand Negroes have joined the movement at one time or another, but few objective observers believe that the Black
Muslims can muster more than twenty or twenty-five thousand active temple people.

THE CONVERTS

The Black Muslims are feverish proselytizers, however, and
they get amazing results from Negro prison inmates and the
abandoned black masses who live in a world of despair and
futility. Early commentators on the movement pointed to
their work among prison inmates as further evidence that
the Black Muslims were a dissolute lot. The opposite has
proved to be true—the Muslims have been able to change
the lives of these men once they emerge from prison. While
the percentage of repeaters among ordinary Negro criminals
runs very high, the Black Muslim converts seldom, if ever,
return to a life of crime.

"Many of my followers—and ministers—were once criminals," Elijah Muhammad boasted in Washington, D.C., "but
I changed all that by giving them knowledge of *self.* Once
they discovered who the devil was and who God was, their
lives were changed."

"All praise due to Allah," the crowd of some five thousand

shouted as they leaped to their feet and applauded with rejoicing.

Non-Muslim Negroes used to scoff when Elijah wrote and talked about "knowledge of self." They are less apt to scoff now that a new wave of race pride has engulfed the Negro and a coterie of clean-cut, well-dressed, polite, and chillingly moral Black Muslim ex-convicts parade through the Negro community each day.

The same general approach, teaching race pride as knowledge of "self," accounts for the success the Black Muslims have among low-income Negroes. For these people are in something of a prison, too; they see themselves as failures and need some accounting for why they are what they are, why they are not what they are not. These needs are met when the wayward and the downtrodden sit at the feet of Malcolm X and hear him proclaim the divinity of the black man, hear him blame the white man for sin and lawlessness and then go on to herald the impending destruction of the "blue-eyed white devil.". . .

MALCOLM'S RELIGION

Dogma and ritual are . . . evidences of the tribalism endemic to religion. I was born and raised a Baptist; long before I could read and write I knew that any person who had not been immersed in water was doomed to Hell. There was nothing to argue about, no need for polemics and reasoning; there would be no Methodists in Heaven!

The point of truth is this: Ethnic and dogmatic bigotry are imbedded in every religious faith plying its wares in the world market; we religious liberals are students of apologetics, sophisticated believers who prefer to forget our crude and tribalistic roots in favor of an enlightened social ethic. Alas, along came Elijah and made us see ourselves as we once were; along came Malcolm X and made us understand what we are now, and why.

The argument that the Black Muslims are not a valid religion because of the exclusivity of their fellowship, then, is clearly spurious. Every religion is a sort of sanctified country club, a coming together of peers in the name of their god. The second argument against the religiosity of the Black Muslims is equally spurious: Like all faiths, the Black Muslims never say hate the other fellow; they say love your own kind. Religious bigotry is Western civilization's major moral blind spot, and Malcolm X has taken up squatters' rights just there.

Thus it is that secularism must save the church—the layman must lead the clergyman to the mourner's bench and make him confess brotherhood in the name of a democratic and pluralistic society. The nature of our social moment demands that we free God from racialism and dogmatics. Racialism, the malignant one of the two cancers, must be dealt with first since it is the prime moral issue of our time. And it must be dealt with by all peoples of all faiths working in concert. Should our social order change, should we somehow come to grips with the evils that have spawned the Black Muslims, the movement would be forced to refine itself or perish.

Malcolm X is the best authority for this. I have often pressed him on his categorical denunciation of the white man as a devil, and his reply is always the same: "The Honorable Elijah Muhammad teaches us that the white man is a devil. We hold to that teaching because history proves the white man is a devil. If he is not a devil," Malcolm X concludes, "then let him prove it. Let him give justice, freedom, and equality to our people."

I have deliberately kept my analysis of the Black Muslims in personal terms of reference because this is precisely how most Negroes feel about the matter—after all, the attraction of the movement for Negroes is one of the major points of this essay. . . .

INTERVIEWING MALCOLM X

LOMAX: Minister Malcolm, we are all by now familiar with your basic philosophy; we have heard you speak, seen you on television, and read your remarks in magazines and newspapers. By now, I think, everybody knows your position that the white man is a devil, a man incapable of doing right; you hold that the black man is of God's divine nature, that he fell from power because of weakness; you hold further that the white man's rule over the earth was scheduled to end in 1914, but that his end has been delayed because of the need to get the American Negro into the fold of black brotherhood.

MALCOLM X: Yes, sir, that is what The Honorable Elijah Muhammad teaches us. The white devil's time is up; it has been up for almost fifty years now. It has taken us that long to get the deaf, dumb, and blind black men in the wilderness of North America to wake up and understand who they are.

You see, sir, when a man understands who he is, who God is, who the devil is . . . then he can pick himself up out of the gutter; he can clean himself up and stand up like a man should before his God. This is why we teach that in order for a man to really understand himself he must be part of a nation; he must have some land of his own, a God of his own, a language of his own. Most of all he must have love and devotion for his own kind.

LOMAX: Wouldn't you say the Negro has a nation—America?

MALCOLM X: Sir, how can a Negro say America is *his* nation? He was brought here in chains; he was put in slavery and worked like a mule for three hundred years; he was separated from his land, his culture, his God, his language!

The Negro was taught to speak the white man's tongue, worship the white God, and accept the white man as his superior.

This is a white man's country, and the Negro is nothing but an ex-slave who is now trying to get himself integrated into the slave master's house.

And the slave master doesn't want you! You fought and bled and died in every war the white man waged, and he still won't give you justice. You nursed his baby and cleaned behind his wife, and he still won't give you freedom; you turned the other cheek while he lynched you and raped your women, but he still won't give you equality. Now, you integration-minded Negroes are trying to force yourselves on your former slave master, trying to make him accept you in his drawing room; you want to hang out with his women rather than with women of your own kind.

LOMAX: Are you suggesting that all of us who fight for integration are after a white woman?

MALCOLM X: I wouldn't say *all* of you, but let the evidence speak for itself. Check up on these integration leaders, and you will find that most of them are either married to or hooked up with some white woman. Take that meeting between James Baldwin and Robert Kennedy; practically everybody there was interracially married. Harry Belafonte is married to a white woman; Lorraine Hansberry is married to a white man; Lena Horne is married to a white man.

Now how can any Negro, man or woman, who sleeps with a white person speak for me? No black person married to a white person can speak for me!

LOMAX: Why?

MALCOLM X: Why? Because only a man who is ashamed of what he is will marry out of his race. There has to be some-

Who Is Louis Lomax?

The name Louis Lomax comes up repeatedly in discussions on the life of Malcolm X. Lomax's fascination with the struggles of poverty-stricken blacks in America kept him coming back repeatedly to Malcolm. Lomax interviewed Malcolm, took notes on him, and followed him to press rallies, until eventually Lomax wrote his own book on Malcolm X and the Nation of Islam. Just who was this man who shadowed Malcolm both during and after his storied life? In Voices from the Sixties, *Pierre Berton gives a brief recounting of the "television prophet" in his own time.*

It is a measure of the change in American attitudes during the Sixties that Louis Lomax has a regular ninety-minute twice-weekly program on a Los Angeles television channel. It is a measure of Lomax's sensitivity that, when one of my researchers approached him in November 1966 and began to ask questions about the civil rights movement, he replied, a bit testily, that he was damned if this was going to be "a Negro interview."

Perhaps he had a special reason that day to be sensitive about his color. A local businessman had just offered him a partnership in a newly formed company—on the insulting condition that he never be seen in public life with a white woman. As Lomax admitted to my researcher, he was still shaking from that experience.

Actually I had no intention of making my interview with Lomax "a Negro interview." Lomax's interests range far beyond the issue of Negro struggle, which he believes to be a mere symptom of a larger American malaise. He is committed to fighting the whole disease rather than eliminating the superficial symptoms one by one.

In this running battle his credentials are impressive. A distinguished writer and reporter, a former assistant professor of philosophy, the holder of two honorary doctorates, he has been named by *Ebony* magazine one of the hundred most influential Negroes in America today. One of his three books, *The Negro Revolt*, is considered the definitive work on the subject. Another, the award-winning *The Reluctant African*, established him as one of the nation's best authorities on the emerging nations.

Pierre Berton, *Voices from the Sixties.* New York: Doubleday, 1967.

thing wrong when a man or a woman leaves his own people and marries somebody of another kind. Men who are proud of being black marry black women; women who are proud of being black marry black men.

This is particularly true when you realize that these Negroes who go for integration and intermarriage are linking up with the very people who lynched their fathers, raped their mothers, and put their kid sisters in the kitchen to scrub floors. Why would any black man in his right mind want to marry a lyncher, a murderer, a rapist, a dope peddler, a gambler, a hog eater . . . Why would any black man want to marry a *devil* . . . for that's just what the white man is. . . .

LOMAX: Minister Malcolm, you often speak of unity among our people. Unity for what?

MALCOLM X: The Honorable Elijah Muhammad teaches us that God now is about to establish a kingdom on this earth based upon brotherhood and peace, and the white man is against brotherhood and the white man is against peace. His history on this earth has proved that. Nowhere in history has he been brotherly toward anyone. The only time he is brotherly toward you is when he can use you, when he can exploit you, when he will oppress you, when you will submit to him, and since his own history makes him unqualified to be an inhabitant or a citizen in the kingdom of brotherhood, The Honorable Elijah Muhammad teaches us that God is about to eliminate that particular race from this earth. Since they are due for elimination, we don't want to be with them. We are not trying to integrate with that which we know has come to the end of its rope. We are trying to separate from it and get with something that is more lasting, and we think that God is more lasting than the white man.

LOMAX: Then your movement does not share the integration goals of the NAACP, CORE, Martin Luther King's movement, and the Student Nonviolent movement.

MALCOLM X: You don't integrate with a sinking ship. You don't do anything to further your stay aboard a ship that you see is going to go down to the bottom of the ocean. Moses tried to separate his people from Pharaoh, and when he tried, the magicians tried to fool the people into staying with Pharaoh, and we look upon these other organizations that are trying to get Negroes to integrate with this doomed white man as nothing but modern-day magicians, and The Honorable Elijah Muhammad is a modern-day Moses trying to separate us from the modern-day Pharaoh. Until the white man in America sits down and talks with The Honorable Elijah Muhammad, he won't even know what the race problem—what makes the race problem what it is. Just like Pharaoh couldn't get a solution to his problem until he talked to Moses, or Nebuchadnezzar or Belshazzar couldn't get a solution to his problem until he talked to Daniel, the white man in America today will never understand the race problem or come anywhere near getting a solution to the race problem until he talks to The Honorable Elijah Muhammad. Mr. Muhammad will give him God's analysis, not some kind of political analysis or psychologist's analysis, or some kind of clergyman's analysis, but God's anaylsis. That's the analysis that Moses gave Pharaoh; that's the analysis that Daniel gave Belshazzar. Today we have a modern Belshazzar and a modern Pharaoh sitting in Washington, D.C.

LOMAX: I am struck by the fact that each of the biblical figures you mentioned—Pharaoh, Nebuchadnezzar, and Belshazzar—came to a rather sorry end. Are you willing to complete the analogy and say the American white establishment will come to a bitter end, perhaps be destroyed?

MALCOLM X: I have spoken on this many times, and I am sure you know what The Honorable Elijah Muhammad teaches on this. But since we are on record I will—as they sometimes say in Harlem—make it plain.

Now, sir, God is going to punish this wicked devil for his misdeeds toward black people. Just as plagues were visited on Pharaoh so will pestilences and disasters be visited on the white man. Why, it has already started: God has begun to send them heat when they expect cold; he sends them cold when they expect heat. Their crops are dying, their children are being born with all kinds of deformities, the rivers and the lakes are coming out of the belly of the earth to wash them away.

Not only that, but God has started slapping their planes down from the sky. Last year [1962] God brought down one of their planes loaded with crackers whose fathers had lynched your and my brothers and sisters. They were from your state, Lomax, down there in Georgia where both you and Mr. Muhammad come from. Now, long before that plane crash I predicted [in Los Angeles] that God was going to strike back at the devil for the way white cops brutalized our brothers in Los Angeles. When the plane fell, I said this was

God's way of letting his wrath be known. I said much the same thing when that submarine—the *Thresher*—went down to the bottom of the sea. Now for this I was called names—some of these Uncle Tom Negroes rushed into print to condemn me for what I had said. But what was wrong with what I said? Everybody has a God and believes that his God will deliver him and protect him from his enemies! Why can't the black man have a God? What's so wrong when a black man says his God will protect him from his white foe? If Jehovah can slay Philistines for the Jews, why can't Allah slay crackers for the so-called Negro? . . .

LOMAX: According to your own newspaper, one of the things you Muslims may *do* in the near future is vote.

MALCOLM X: Yes. After long and prayerful consideration, The Honorable Elijah Muhammad allowed us to announce the possibility of Muslims voting. The announcement came at our annual Saviour's Day convention in Chicago.

LOMAX: What does it mean?

MALCOLM X: Mr. Muhammad is the only one who can explain that fully. However, I can say that we may register and be ready to vote. Then we will seek out candidates who represent our interests and support them. They need not be Muslims; what we want are race men who will speak out for our people.

LOMAX: There are rumors that you may run against Adam Clayton Powell.

MALCOLM X: Why must I run against a Negro? We have had enough of Negroes running against and fighting each other. The better bet is that we would put a Muslim candidate in the field against a devil, somebody who is against all we stand for.

LOMAX: What are the chances of the Black Muslims joining us in picket lines for better jobs? . . .

MALCOLM X: As I told you, only Mr. Muhammad can answer that. But let me tell you something: Better jobs and housing are only temporary solutions. They are aspects of tokenism and don't go to the heart of the problem.

This is why integration will not work. It assumes that the two races, black and white, are equal and can be made to live as one. This is not true.

The white man is by nature a devil and must be destroyed. The black man will inherit the earth; he will resume control, taking back the position he held centuries ago when the white devil was crawling around the caves of Europe on his all fours. Before the white devil came into our lives we had a civilization, we had a culture, we were living in silks and satins. Then he put us in chains and placed us aboard the "Good Ship Jesus," and we have lived in hell ever since.

Now the white man's time is over. Tokenism will not help him, and it will doom us. Complete separation will save us— and who knows, it might make God decide to give the white devil a few more years.

The Fanatic and His Subversive Cult

Clayborne Carson

Clayborne Carson, a Stanford researcher and lecturer, uncovered the extensive file on Malcolm X made by the FBI. The following is an excerpt from Carson's *Malcolm X: The FBI File*, a reproduction of FBI writings with comments from Carson. The FBI was then composed entirely of white Americans under J. Edgar Hoover, who was often criticized for being racist. As a result, the file, written by anonymous FBI personnel, refers to Malcolm as a "fanatic," a man with deep psychological problems. It reduces the Nation of Islam to a "Muslim cult" and focuses on Malcolm's more far-fetched statements (even noting Malcolm's claim that the Nation was in control of a weapons station in space).

Although the FBI under the leadership of J. Edgar Hoover was consistently hostile toward African-American militancy, the federal government's policies toward the Nation of Islam were inconsistent. The FBI's surveillance of Elijah Muhammad and his followers prior to the 1960s did not result from a widely shared perception among government officials that the Nation of Islam was subversive. Instead, it resulted from the determination of Hoover and other FBI officials to continue surveillance even without explicit authority. The Nation's potential as a stimulus for revolutionary and seditious activities became evident to the FBI mainly as a result of the increasing prominence of Malcolm X and the increasing militancy and scale of black protests.

While Hoover and other Bureau officials saw the group as one of many types of subversive black militancy, other officials of the Justice Department were not convinced that the Muslims represented a serious threat. The 1975 Church Committee hearings on intelligence activities included a summary of the discussions between the FBI and Justice Department officials regarding the Nation of Islam. In 1952, the Bureau suggested adding the Muslims to the Attorney General's list of subversive organizations, and the following year the Department of Justice concluded that the Nation of Islam would not be prosecuted under the anticommunist Smith Act but decided that "the group would under certain circumstances represent a serious threat to our national security." In 1954, the Justice Department decided against prosecuting the Nation for conspiracy to violate the Selective Service Act. In 1955, the Justice officials responded inconclusively to the FBI's request for advice on whether Muslim activists should remain on the Security Index. In 1959, the Department indicated to Hoover that it did not support prosecution of the Nation or designation on the Attorney General's list. In 1960, according to testimony before the Church Committee, the Department advised that the group was

> not subversive as defined by the employee security program. However, the FBI was requested to continue its investigation of the group.

> Hoover noted on the bottom of that memorandum, after he received it, that Justice was "just stalling."

During the 1960s, Justice Department officials questioned whether Elijah Muhammad's prophesies constitute subversive threats but did not request that the FBI discontinue its investigation of the Nation of Islam. Without explicit instructions from Justice Department officials, the FBI continued to compile information on the Muslims until after the death of Elijah Muhammad.

The following documents are selected from the large body of FBI records that refer to Malcolm X. They have been edited to eliminate repetitive material and some material from non-FBI sources, such as newspaper articles on Malcolm X. The Bureau opened its file on Malcolm X shortly after his release from prison in March, 1953 and in 1958 designated him "a key figure" as a result of his increasing national visibility. Even after his assassination, the Bureau continued to refer to Malcolm in its reports, especially after 1966, when the Bureau broadened [its] focus. . . from leftist organizations to include "Black nationalist-hate groups."

The file is divided into 19 sections, chronologically arranged. Included in the reports are Malcolm's personal correspondence, reports of speeches and sermons, and transcripts of radio and television interviews.

Before releasing this file, the Federal Bureau of Investigation deleted numerous passages in accordance with exemptions allowed under the Freedom of Information Act. The specific reasons for many deleted passages are indicated by the references to subsections of Title 5, United States Code, Section 552. Thus, deleted sections with the following references were withheld because they were deemed to meet the following criteria:

b2   —related solely to the internal personnel rules and practices of an agency.

b7   —(c) could reasonably be expected to constitute an unwarranted invasion of personal privacy.

—(d) could reasonably be expected to disclose the identity of a confidential source, including a State, local, or foreign agency or authority or any private institution which furnished information on a confidential basis, and, in the case of a record or information compiled by a criminal law enforcement authority in the course of a criminal investigation, or by an agency conducted a lawful national security intelligence investigation, information furnished by a confidential source. . . .

FILE EXTRACTS

MUSLIM CULT OF ISLAM

[BUREAU DELETION] the Muslim Cult of Islam, which is also known as the Allah Temple of Islam, is a religious cult whose members regard Allah as their supreme being and claim to be the direct descendants of the original race on earth. The members fanatically follow the teachings of Allah as interpreted by ELIJAH MUHAMMAD, the "true prophet of Allah" entitled titular head of the Muslim Cult of Islam in the United States, and believe that any civil law which conflicts with the Muslim law should be disobeyed. The members disavow their allegiance to the United States and pledge their allegiance only to Allah and do not consider it their duty to register for Selective Service or to serve in the United States Armed Forces as they cannot serve two masters. According to the teachings of ELIJAH MUHAMMAD and the cult's ministers, the members of a minority race in the United States are not citizens of this country but are merely slaves of this country and will continue to be slaves until they free themselves by destroying non-Muslims and Christianity in the "War of Armageddon."

[BUREAU DELETION] the cult teaches that the Korean War is a futile effort by the United States to prevent the coming Asiatic conquest of the world and the defeat of the United States in Korea is a prelude to the "resurrection" when North America and Great Britain will be doomed and the original man, led by Allah, will reign supreme.

[BUREAU DELETION] the following information taken from another letter of Subject of January 29, 1950:

> It is better to be jailed by the devil for serving Allah than it is to be allowed by the devil to walk free. The black man has been enslaved. The time is coming for the devils to be destroyed. . . .

FEDERAL BUREAU OF INVESTIGATION
This case originated at: Detroit, Michigan
Report made at: Detroit, Michigan
Date when made: 3/16/54 . . .

Title: CHANGED:
MALCOLM K. LITTLE, was Malachi Shabazz; "Rhythm Red"; "Detroit Red"; Jack Carlton; Malcolm X Little
Character of case: Security Matter-C; Security Matter-MCI

SUMMARY REPORT:
Subject presently traveling about United States making contacts with various temples of the Muslim Cult of Islam. Receives mail at 18887 Keystone, Detroit, Michigan. Subject, [BUREAU DELETION] wrote letters indicating he was a Communist. [BUREAU DELETION] Subject wrote letters indicating membership in Muslim Cult of Islam. Subject reported in attendance at various Muslim Cult of Islam meetings in Detroit from February, 1953 to June, 1953. Criminal record and description set out.

The title of this case is being marked changed to include the alias *Malcolm X Little*, by which name the Subject is known in the Muslim Cult of Islam.

FEDERAL BUREAU OF INVESTIGATION
This case originated at: Philadelphia
Report made at: New York
Date when made: 9/7/54 . . .
DETAILS:
Brother MALCOLM LITTLE of the Cult's Temple at Boston, Massachusetts was a guest speaker at the Muslim

Cult of Islam (MCI) meeting on January 8, 1954. [BUREAU DELETION] the subject had suggested that all members start a recruitment of younger members to go to the future meetings of the MCI. . . .

[BUREAU DELETION] MALCOLM X had stated that he had recently been transferred from the Philadelphia area to replace the former minister who had traveled from Washington to handle the duties of the minister in the New York area. He advised that MALCOLM X appeared to be more ed-ucated than other members of the cult and was a very convincing speaker. He advised that during the course of some of the subject's talks, he had openly spoken against the "white devils" and had encouraged greater hatred on the part of the cult towards the white race.

[BUREAU DELETION] during one of the sermons given by MALCOLM X, he told the audience that he had once served in a federal penitentiary and stated that he was quite proud of the fact that he was chosen to serve time in the federal penitentiary for his beliefs in the Muslim doctrine. [BUREAU DELETION] the subject had encouraged the members to deem it an honor and a privilege to be called upon by the prophet to spend time in the federal penitentiary because of their religious beliefs. . . .

FEDERAL BUREAU OF INVESTIGATION
This case originated at: New York
Report made at: New York
Date when made: 1/25/55 . . .

Service in the Armed Forces
[BUREAU DELETION] MALCOLM LITTLE had regis-tered at Local Board 59 of New York City on June 1, 1943 while residing at 2460 Seventh Avenue, Apartment 31, New York City. [BUREAU DELETION] on October 25, 1943 the subject was found mentally disqualified for military service for the following reasons: psychopathic personality inade-quate, sexual perversion, psychiatric rejection. Subject was classified 4F on December 4, 1944. . . .

Information Concerning the Muslim Cult of Islam (MCI)
[BUREAU DELETION] the MCI, also known as the Tem-ple of Islam and the Allah Temple of Islam, is an organiza-tion composed entirely of Negroes, which was reportedly or-

ganized around 1930 in Detroit, Michigan. The national leader and founder is ELIJAH MUHAMMAD, who claims to have been sent by ALLAH, the supreme being, to lead the Negroes out of slavery in the United States.

Members fanatically follow the alleged teachings of AL-LAH, as interpreted by MUHAMMAD, and disavow allegiance to the United States. Members pledge allegiance only to ALLAH and Islam and believe any civil law which conflicts with Muslim law should be disobeyed. The Cult teaches that members of the dark-skinned race cannot be considered citizens of the United States since they are in slavery in this country, and, therefore, must free themselves by destroying non-Muslims and Christianity in the "War of Armageddon." For this purpose, the Cult has a military branch called the Fruit of Islam (FOI) composed of all-male, able-bodied members, who participate in military drill and judo training.

Members of the Cult also believe that they are directly related to all Asiatic races, and any conflict involving any Asiatic nation and a Western nation is considered a part of the War of Armageddon, in which the Asiatic nation will be victorious. . . .

[BUREAU DELETION] MALCOLM LITTLE was the main speaker at the MCI meeting. [BUREAU DELETION] that LITTLE spoke about the "white man" as being the "devil" and made statements that the United States government could pass a bill overnight but cannot even pass a "civil rights bill" in years. LITTLE claimed that all the "white devils" are being chased out of Asia by the "black man" and that they are all coming to the United States.

LITTLE told this group that there was a space ship forty miles up which was built by the wise men of the East and in this space ship there are a number of smaller space ships and each one is loaded with bombs. LITTLE stated that when ELIJAH MUHAMMAD of Chicago, Illinois, gives the word these ships will descend on the United States, bomb it and destroy all the "white devils." According to LITTLE these bombs will destroy all the "devils" in the United States and that all the Muslims in good standing will be spared. LITTLE claimed that their Prophet ELIJAH MUHAMMAD was sent to the United States twenty years ago to save the "black people."

Leaving the Nation of Islam

Jim Haskins

Malcolm was brought into the Nation partly because
of his talent for oratory. But it was that same talent,
the fiery temperament and the strength of Malcolm's
voice, that in the end forced him to leave. His faith in
the leaders of Islam deteriorated when he discovered
some sexual indiscretions on the part of his mentor,
Elijah Muhammad. As trust eroded between Malcolm and Muhammad, Malcolm feared he might be
permanently silenced for his dissension and his own
popularity within the Nation. Jim Haskins talks
about those last few fateful years that Malcolm spent
in New York before leaving the Nation of Islam to
start his own church. Haskins is a well-published
author. A large portion of his more than eighty books
has been written on the subject of African American
culture. He has won the Coretta Scott King Honor
Book award and teaches at the University of Florida.

Malcolm X found the worldly-wise and weary residents of
Harlem difficult to approach. In the early months, he was
continually frustrated. But he kept on. His single-mindedness
about advancing the cause of the Nation was disturbed during this period when he fell in love with Sister Betty X, born
Betty Sanders, who joined Temple No. 7 in 1956. A nurse,
she taught Muslim Girls Training classes one night a week
after her normal work at a local hospital. She and Malcolm
X were married in January 1958, and in the next six years
would have four daughters. . . .

[Meanwhile,] from Harlem, word about the Muslims
spread quickly to the rest of the city. It was not long before
Mike Wallace, then a young television news reporter who
had a program called "Newsbeat" on local television station

Jim Haskins, *Louis Farrakhan and the Nation of Islam.* New York: Walker and Company, 1996. Copyright © 1996 by Walker and Company. Reproduced by permission.

WNTA, became interested in the Nation. With Louis Lomax, a black veteran news reporter, as chief researcher, Wallace undertook an investigation of the Nation of Islam. The program aired on July 10, 1959, and included footage taken at mosques and Muslim-owned-and-operated restaurants in New York, Chicago, and Washington, D.C., as well as clips of a performance of Minister Louis X's [play] *The Trial* before an audience of 2,000 black people at Boston's John Hancock Hall. The program also presented excerpts from Elijah Muhammad's speeches and those of other ministers, including Malcolm X, and an interview with Malcolm X that Louis Lomax conducted after flying to Chicago to secure Elijah Muhammad's consent.

A REPORT ON HATE

The program was called "The Hate That Hate Produced," a title suggesting that white hatred of blacks had produced black hatred in response. But its emphasis was on the anti-white teachings of the Nation of Islam. Malcolm X complained later that every phrase he had uttered in his interview had been edited to produce the greatest shock value. Whether or not the program presented a balanced picture of the Muslims, it sent shock waves through New York, whose white newspaper editors and columnists sounded the alarm about this group of black segregationists and black supremacists. From there, the national newsmagazines carried the story to the rest of the country; soon, the Nation of Islam was nationwide news. . . .

As Minister of Temple No. 7 in New York, the media capital of the world, Malcolm X was the representative of the Nation of Islam to whom reporters turned most often for responses to what the rest of the country was saying. After discussing what he should say with Elijah Muhammad in Chicago, he responded with the fury he felt: "For the white man to ask the black man if he hates him is just like the rapist asking the *raped*, or the wolf asking the *sheep*, 'Do you hate me?' The white man is in no moral *position* to accuse anyone else of hate!". . .

MORE PUBLIC EXPOSURE

In 1961, two years after "The Hate That Hate Produced" aired on New York television, C. Eric Lincoln's book *The Black Muslims in America* was published. Lincoln, who in

1956 was teaching religion and philosophy at Clark College in Atlanta, Georgia, had been struck by a student's paper on the incompatibility of the Christian religion with the black man's aspirations for dignity and equality in America. On questioning the student, he learned that the young man had come under the influence of the local Muslim minister. Lincoln undertook a study of the Nation of Islam and produced the first book about the movement. The term "Black Muslims" was Lincoln's; Elijah Muhammad, Malcolm X, and other Muslim ministers took great pains to correct the impression that they called themselves Black Muslims: They were black *people.* They were properly called Muslims. But the name stuck.

The Black Muslims in America inspired another huge response from the public, and once again Malcolm X was thrown into the spotlight as the official spokesman of the Nation of Islam and its National Minister.

The Nation of Islam benefited from all the publicity generated by "The Hate That Hate Produced" and *The Black Muslims in America.* Taking advantage of the increased recognition, Elijah Muhammad appeared at a number of mass rallies in cities with Muslim temples; caravans of buses carried the Muslim faithful to the rallies. Thousands attended, and many more were unable to fit inside; huge speakers were set up outside the rallies so they could hear the speeches.

Malcolm X was always present; his role was to prime the crowd before he introduced the Honorable Elijah Muhammad. So were his brothers, Wilfred, minister of the temple in Detroit, and Philbert, minister of the temple in Lansing, Michigan, and Elijah Muhammad's son, Wallace Muhammad, minister of the Philadelphia Temple. By this time, there were also temples in Los Angeles; Atlantic City; Washington, D.C.; Camden, New Jersey; Richmond, Virginia; Hartford, Connecticut; and Buffalo, New York. Louis X was one of the youngest ministers, but he was not the only one who had grown up middle class. One minister was a former Christian cleric; another was a pathologist. They reflected the increasingly middle-class membership of the Nation of Islam. . . .

CLASH WITH BLACK CHRISTIANS

Except in Atlanta, the South's largest city, the Nation of Islam had made few inroads in the South. Southern blacks, subjected to the cruelest forms of segregation, were also, as a group, the most strongly Christian. They believed that America could be better and that through the application of Christian principles and nonviolent protest tactics, they could overcome the hatred that festered in white souls. While the Nation of Islam was holding mass rallies in northern cities, Martin Luther King, Jr.'s, Southern Christian Leadership Conference, the Congress of Racial Equality, the Student Nonviolent Coordinating Committee, and the National Association for the Advancement of Colored People were conducting Freedom Rides to test laws against segregation on interstate bus travel, voter registration drives and marches for voting rights, and boycotts of businesses that discriminated against blacks.

A. Philip Randolph, founder of the Brotherhood of Sleeping Car Porters, the first African-American labor union, believed the time had come for a massive March on Washington for Jobs and Freedom. He managed to persuade the leaders of the major civil rights organizations to support the march, and brought in white labor and church leaders as well. Scheduled for August 28, 1963, the march was planned to be the largest peacetime demonstration in U.S. history.

The Nation of Islam would not be participating. Malcolm X voiced the Nation's belief that the major civil rights leaders were but "puppets" of the administration of President John F. Kennedy and that the march was really a pep rally in support of the president. Two days before the march, Malcolm X arrived in Washington, D.C., and announced that he would hold a press conference to explain his views on what he called the "Farce on Washington." The conference was to be held August 27, on the evening before the march.

Worried that if he denounced the march on the eve of the event he might succeed in persuading some people to stay away, the civil rights leaders met with Malcolm X and asked him not to hold the planned press conference on August 27, arguing that he would be going against the entire black community if he did. Malcolm X agreed not to hold the press conference as originally planned. He did hold a press conference during the march, and did indeed denounce it. But because of the rescheduling, the conference did not affect participation in the march; nor was the conference well-attended, because most reporters were covering the march itself. The march was a huge success, attracting at least a quarter of a million people, black and white, and making a powerful statement to America and its elected representatives in the nation's capital. In less than two years, laws would be passed that would effectively end legal segregation in the United States.

Malcolm X had compromised his own position for the good of the black community. He had not been in the habit of doing so. But by 1963, he had come to recognize some deep divisions between his beliefs in what the Nation of Islam could become and what Elijah Muhammad wanted it to be.

MALCOLM'S DISENCHANTMENT

In the view of Malcolm X, the Nation had the potential to use its numbers and influence to right the wrongs committed against blacks by white society. But that was contrary to Elijah Muhammad's strict policy of nonengagement. Malcolm had heard the Muslims criticized because they talked tough but never *did* anything, and part of him agreed with that sentiment. Muslims were not to vote or engage in any types of political activity or civil rights demonstrations. In Boston, Minister Louis X severely criticized a temple member just for joining a community group that protested police brutality against African-Americans. In doing so, Louis X was toeing the anti-engagement line established by Elijah Muhammad. Malcolm X's sister, Ella, had left the Boston Muslim temple in 1959, partly because its leaders refused to participate in activities that she felt would benefit the community.

Far more serious than this disagreement over tactics, however, were events that occurred in the early 1960s—events that shook Malcolm X's faith in himself, in Elijah Muhammad, and in the Nation of Islam. Ever since he had become a national figure, Malcolm X had been aware of growing jealousy of him within the movement. Elijah Muhammad continued to support and encourage him to his face, but the younger man was aware that privately Elijah Muhammad might be concerned that he was becoming too popular. If Malcolm X's faith in Elijah Muhammad had not been shaken at that time, he might have been able to withstand the jealousy and bad feeling. But Malcolm X was beginning to be convinced that rumors he had heard since as far back as 1955 might be true. It was whispered that Elijah Muhammad, in addition to fathering nine children by his wife, had also fathered several children by various secretaries over the years. In July 1962, two of his former secretaries filed paternity suits against him.

There was no stronger prohibition in the Nation of Islam than that against adultery. It was difficult for Malcolm X to believe that the man he had idolized all these years could have committed such a sin. Even when he learned for himself that the charges were true, Malcolm X could not turn his back on his mentor. With the help of Wallace Muhammad, Elijah Muhammad's son, Malcolm reviewed the Qu'ran and the Bible to remind himself that other important figures in religious history, such as David and Lot, had committed similar sins. Malcolm X told himself, and began to teach at Temple No. 7, that a man's accomplishments outweighed his personal, human weaknesses.

But the rumors continued. They were especially rife in Chicago and Detroit, where the Nation of Islam began to lose members, and where some non-Muslim blacks were becoming adamantly anti-Muslim. Before the rumors reached the East Coast, Malcolm X decided he had better prepare some of the ministers there. He was in for a surprise. As he recalled in his autobiography, "I found then that some of them had already heard of it; one of them, Minister Louis X of Boston, as much as seven months before. They had been living with the dilemma themselves."

DEPARTURE

Then, on November 22, 1963, President John F. Kennedy was felled by an assassin's bullet while riding in a motorcade in Dallas, Texas. The nation was in shock. Elijah Muhammad immediately sent out a directive that no Muslim minister was to make any comment whatsoever on the assassination. Malcolm X fully expected to obey that directive. But then Elijah Muhammad canceled a planned speech in New York City and asked Malcolm X to take his place. After the speech, a reporter asked him his opinion on the president's assassination, and without thinking, he responded that white people's hate had finally cut down the nation's president, that it was a case of "the chickens coming home to roost." The next day, that remark screamed from news headlines and news broadcasts. At his regularly scheduled monthly meeting with Elijah Muhammad that same day, Malcolm X learned that his remark would have an adverse effect on all Muslims and that he was to be silenced for the next ninety days. He was not to talk to the press, or teach at Temple No. 7. Louis X was named National Minister in his place.

Malcolm X soon understood that he would never regain the support and trust of Elijah Muhammad. He learned that one of his own assistant ministers was saying he should be killed, and he knew that in the tightly disciplined world of the Nation, such talk could have been approved by only one man. After a trusted assistant told him of a plan to wire the ignition of his car with a bomb, Malcolm X knew his time in the Nation of Islam was over. He announced that he was leaving the Nation.

While his faith in Elijah Muhammad was shattered, Malcolm X continued to believe in many of the tenets of the Muslim faith he had learned. He still believed in Allah. He called a press conference in New York and announced that he was forming a new organization, called Muslim Mosque, Inc., with temporary headquarters at the Hotel Theresa in Harlem.

CHAPTER 4

ASSASSINATION

MALCOLM X

Malcolm Pursued and Killed

Bruce Perry

Malcolm's role as leader of his own project, the Muslim Mosque, would turn out to be short-lived. After leaving the Nation of Islam, Malcolm was outspoken about the problems he saw with Elijah Muhammad's leadership. Malcolm's former mentor was livid. As a prominent spokesman, Malcolm was still desired by rally-makers and organizers of black unity events across the United States. However, the Nation of Islam—and Muhammad in particular—stood against him. Meanwhile, the FBI and other government agencies tightened their surveillance of Malcolm, who was still considered a subversive. Feeling the pressure, Malcolm soon recognized that he was in serious danger, and that enemies old and new were plotting against him. Bruce Perry's intensive research on Malcolm X gives a good summary of the events leading up to Malcolm's assassination in 1965.

The first issue of *Muhammad Speaks* that appeared in 1965 contained the conciliatory pronouncement that disbelievers "are to be forgiven if they renounce hypocrisy." There was also a declaration that Allah "specifically chooses for his mercy whom he pleases." Yet, in the next issue, Elijah Muhammad [often called "the Messenger" by his people] dwelled at considerable length on the fate of "hypocrites." He singled out Malcolm, whom he called "the Chief Hypocrite," for particular criticism. "He has said everything imaginable against me," Muhammad declared. "I will never forget." Though he predicted "painful chastisement" for those who defied him, he admonished his followers not to kill them. The admonition was apparently necessary; one believer told Charles Kenyatta, "You fell in love with that red nigger, but we're going to kill him."

The January 15 issue of the Nation of Islam's newspaper suggested that the Nation of Islam (NOI) leadership was divided about how to proceed on the Malcolm issue. In a column entitled "From The Messenger," the following passage appeared:

> You and I have arrived at a day of decision. We have come to the crossroads—the point where we must make a decision on what we shall do.

Identical language appeared in an accompanying editorial. That same week, Akbar Muhammad announced that he had quit the Nation of Islam. He said he could no longer abide his father's "concocted religious teachings, which are . . . in most cases diametrically opposed to Islam." Akbar, whom *Muhammad Speaks* dubbed the "Little Hypocrite," indicated that he sympathized with many of Malcolm's views. Eight days later, Malcolm, whom the NOI blamed for Akbar's defection, was reportedly attacked in front of his Queens home. He told one newsman there were three assailants. The number eventually grew to five or six. "I came out with my talking stick," he told the *Amsterdam News.* He told one questioner he had thrashed his attackers.

By this time, violent reprisals against dissidents had become established practice in the Nation of Islam. The preceding December, a number of Malcolm's Philadelphia followers had been assaulted by ten or fifteen members of Elijah Muhammad's Philadelphia temple. The same week, Leon 4X Ameer, who described himself, accurately or otherwise, as Malcolm's New England organizer, was clubbed to his knees in the lobby of Boston's Sherry Biltmore Hotel by the captain of Elijah's Boston temple and three other Black Muslims. An armed detective who happened to be in a shop inside the hotel dashed out and rescued Ameer. But, later the same night, another pack forced its way into his hotel room. Battering his face to a pulp, they fractured a number of his ribs and ruptured both his eardrums. The following day, he was discovered, unconscious, in the bathtub. He was rushed to Boston City Hospital, where he lay in a coma with a blood clot on the brain. He emerged from the hospital a semi-invalid. . . .

HOUNDING MALCOLM

The attacks on . . . Ameer and others underscored a late-January prediction by *Muhammad Speaks* that 1965 would be "a year in which the most outspoken opponents of the Honorable Elijah Muhammad will slink into ignoble silence." But Malcolm, who had vowed to tame the pseudo-Islamic monster that was devouring its own adherents, had no intention of keeping silent. The day before the NOI newspaper published its ominous prophecy, he flew to California, ostensibly to establish an Organization of Afro-American Unity (OAAU) chapter in Los Angeles and to "look after" [Muhammad's ex-lovers] Heather and Robin. But no organizational meeting was held. Instead, Malcolm escorted the two women to Gladys Towles Root's law office. Without being asked, he volunteered to testify in their behalf, presumably about Elijah Muhammad's admission that he had fathered a number of illegitimate children. Though he had never spent a day in law school—or even high school—he seemed thoroughly cognizant of the fact that, if the paternity suits ever came to trial, his testimony would likely prove decisive. (Uncorroborated, Heather's and Robin's story might not have been believed.)

The visit to Mrs. Root's office was the third or fourth Malcolm had made. "He was frightened," she later recalled. Malcolm, who asked her if she had inadvertently disclosed his involvement in the proceedings, had every reason to be apprehensive; everywhere he went in Los Angeles, he was hounded by Elijah's followers. The official in charge of the surveillance was apparently John Ali, who was on hand at Los Angeles airport when Malcolm arrived there. The minister and the captain of the Los Angeles mosque even showed up at the Statler Hilton, where Malcolm stopped briefly before meeting with Mrs. Root. In fact, Malcolm ran into the two men at the top of one of the hotel escalators. The mouth of one of them curled up at the side, almost like a dog baring its fangs. "They wanted to kill Malcolm . . . right there," his companion Hakim Jamal later recalled. . . .

The following day, on the way to the airport, two automobiles filled with NOI men gave chase. As one car tried to pull abreast, Malcolm grabbed a cane and poked it out the window, as if it were a rifle. The pursuing vehicle dropped back. Malcolm's car sped on to the airport. . . .

Hours later, when Malcolm arrived in Chicago, policemen were present. They escorted him to his hotel and took up residence in the room next to his. Malcolm had not requested the police protection and appeared suspicious of the motives of the officers. But after Sergeant Ed McClellan, whose men treated Malcolm with deference, explained that they were there to help, Malcolm warmed up considerably. . . .

While Malcolm was in Chicago, he was interviewed by the television talk-show host Irv Kupcinet, who asked how he felt about the argument that the Black Muslim movement was not a bona fide religion. Malcolm conceded that it might be a religion but said it was not the real Islam. As he prepared to leave the television station, he noticed one of Elijah Muhammad's followers in the lobby. Outside, a Volkswagen truck pulled out in front of the unmarked police car that had been waiting for him. Ten or more tough-looking black men began converging on it. The police kept back the attackers, who may have been prompted by reports that the Illinois Attorney General was scrutinizing the Nation of Islam's tax-exemptions. When Malcolm returned to his hotel, he spotted another swarm of NOI men. "Elijah seems to know every move I make," he told Sergeant McClellan. Moments later he added, "It's only going to be a matter of time before they catch up with me.". . .

Malcolm dug his own grave deeper by announcing, back in New York, that he planned to expose Elijah Muhammad's flirtation with the Ku Klux Klan, which, like the Nation of Islam, advocated racial separation. Five days later, *Muhammad Speaks* published the following statement by one of Elijah's "personal" secretaries:

> Throughout the years, I have witnessed the birth and death of many ministers.

The remainder of the article assailed Malcolm and defended Elijah. Elsewhere in the same issue, another spokesman attacked Malcolm. He predicted that the time was coming when the opposition would be dealt a final, crushing blow. "Soon . . . you will see," he declared. In the following issue (which devoted considerable space to Malcolm), he said it was too late for Malcolm to retract all the bitter seeds he had sown. On another page, the Messenger—who had reportedly proclaimed that Malcolm was destroying himself—announced that the so-called Chief Hypocrite had "stepped beyond the limits." "I am no more to suffer," he said. Malcolm apparently understood what he meant; he told [editor] Alex Haley he wanted to read the manuscript of his autobiography one more time because he didn't expect to read it in finished form. He also told Haley, "Each day I live as if I am already dead.". . .

POLITICAL IRRELEVANCE

For the time being, Malcolm contented himself with verbal broadsides against political targets such as George Lincoln Rockwell, the fuehrer of the American Nazi Party. Rockwell ... had been outmaneuvered by National States Rights Party leader Jimmy George Robinson, who had stolen the show by luring Martin Luther King into a conversation that ended when he slugged King. Malcolm, who saw the incident on television, sent a telegram threatening "maximum physical retaliation" if anyone else was hurt. He gave the press a copy of the telegram, which one of his aides apparently sent to Rockwell instead of Robinson. But the press did not accord it prominence. About a week later, Malcolm told an interviewer that it was easy for outsiders to stand on the political sidelines making militant-sounding pronouncements. Outwardly, the remark was a critique of an ultra-leftist publication that had accused him of reaching an accommodation with the establishment. But perhaps it was also a self-critique. He told a group of Mississippi youths who had distinguished themselves in the civil rights struggle:

> How do you think I feel to have to tell you, "We, my generation, sat around like a knot on a wall while the whole world was fighting for its human rights . . . . What did we do, who preceded you? I'll tell you what we did: Nothing."

Malcolm said he wanted a "real" revolution, as opposed to what he characterized as James Baldwin's "pseudo-revolt." He intimated that Martin Luther King was the one who lacked a political program.

But the rapidly approaching culmination of the civil rights movement rendered such rhetoric increasingly immaterial. Malcolm's growing political irrelevance, which he tried to conceal with claims that he had been offered jobs by Nasser and Nkrumah, made it difficult for him to carve out a niche for himself in the rapidly changing political landscape. The alternative was to seek meaning in the personal realm. But, despite his assertions to the contrary, Malcolm never had been able to maintain close personal attachments.

Thus, despite his political genius, Malcolm had little reason for optimism. At times, he seemed terribly dejected. His shoes, which he had always taken such great care to shine, were unpolished and unkempt. Some associates sensed that he still regretted severing his ties with the Nation of Islam. One of them was Christine Johnson. "His heart was still with the movement," she later recalled. "He had given everything for the Nation. After he left it, he had nothing to live for. He didn't care whether he lived or died."

AN INTERNATIONAL PLOT

During the eleven months that had elapsed since Malcolm had severed his relationship with the Nation of Islam, he had been abroad six months. Nevertheless, on Friday, February 5, the same day Martin Luther King and his associates renewed their carefully-planned Selma campaign, Malcolm left once again for Europe. Before he departed, he announced that he would reveal a bold, militant action-program at an OAAU rally February 15. Earlier, he had promised it for January.

On Monday, February 8, Malcolm addressed the Council of African Organizations in London. On Tuesday, while en route to Geneva, he flew to Paris to address the Federation of African Students. But at Orly Airport, he was detained by French immigration officials, whose superiors were reportedly upset by a speech he had given in Paris the previous November. The Interior Ministry announced that his presence in France, which has a sizable black population, was "undesirable."

The immigration authorities, who feared that Malcolm's presence might provoke the kind of racial disturbances that England was beginning to experience, would not even let him telephone the people who had planned to meet him at the airport. Nor would they allow him to call the American embassy. They hinted that the U.S. State Department had asked them to bar him from France. Malcolm admitted that he didn't know whether this was true. The likelihood was remote that de Gaulle's government, which was doing everything it could to stress its independence from the United States, had yielded to American pressure on an issue that didn't even involve the U.S.

Yet, as time passed, Malcolm appeared to put increasing stock in the thesis that he was the target of an international conspiracy. "This thing is bigger than Chicago," he told one associate. "I know what they can do and what they can't," he told another. Ella also subscribed to the thesis that he was the victim of an international plot.

The French authorities kept Malcolm under guard at the airport. After a while, Malcolm dug into his pocket, fished out an English penny, and handed it to one of the gendarmes.

"Give that to de Gaulle," he said, "because the French government is worth less than a penny." The gendarme declined the coin. Malcolm flung it to the floor. Minutes later, he was bundled onto a plane back to England. Whether he managed to get to Geneva is unclear; he had scheduled a visit to the city's "Islamic Center," according to a cablegram the American Legation in Paris addressed to J. Edgar Hoover. (The quotation marks were the legation's.) The Center, which was headed by Said Ramadan, worked closely with Surrur Sabban's Islamic World League. Ramadan and his associates urged the League and its Saudi backers to aid Malcolm financially.

FIRE

Two days after Malcolm was barred from France, he spoke at the London School of Economics. He also gave a speech in Birmingham. Afterwards, the BBC invited him to accompany a team of reporters to a suburb of Birmingham named Smethwick, which was experiencing a large influx of "colored" immigrants.

Smethwick's whites were fleeing the town, which was seething with racial tension. The BBC unsuccessfully tried to arrange a face-to-face confrontation between Malcolm and a Conservative member of Parliament from Smethwick named Peter Griffiths, who had recently unseated a leading Labor Party M.P. with the help of anonymous leaflets that read, "If you want a nigger neighbour, vote Liberal or Labour." The refrain became so popular that it was reportedly taken up by children, who sang it in the streets.

Malcolm returned to New York on Saturday, February 13, the day after the Nation of Islam's lawyers petitioned the authorities to oust him from his home, which Judge Wahl had ordered him to vacate by January 31. . . .

At about 2:30 A.M. on the fourteenth . . . a taxi driver drove by Malcolm's East Elmhurst home and saw something ablaze in a small tree that stood adjacent to two porch windows. The driver stopped, leaped from his cab, and beat out the flames with his clipboard. No one else was in sight except his passenger, who drew his attention to flames emanating from a living-room window on the south side of the house—flames neither man had noticed when the taxi had approached the house from that direction. Both men rushed to the front door to warn the occupants. Inside, they heard

On the morning of February 14, 1965, Malcolm's home was fire-bombed. Members of the Nation were among the suspects caught by police.

yelling and glass breaking, but no one came to the front door. They decided to return to the cab and look for the nearest fire alarm box. As the cab driver re-entered his taxi, he spotted, in the rear yard, another fire—a blaze he hadn't seen when he had alighted from his cab to douse the first one. There was still no one else in sight.

When the fire engines reached the burning house, fireman John McLaughlin found Malcolm standing outside in a white robe and a black Russian hat. Fireman Kenneth Kopp was struck by the fact that he was smiling. . . .

A few hours after the fire engines departed, Malcolm flew to Detroit and told a gathering:

> I was in a house, last night, that was bombed. My own! But I d . . . [Malcolm stopped and changed the word "I" to "It."] It didn't destroy all my clothes.

Privately, he charged the Nation of Islam with responsibility for the fire. Initially, he limited his public response to a declaration that "supporters" of the movement might have set the blaze. But, on Monday, February 15, he placed the blame squarely on the Messenger's shoulders. He candidly admitted that he was "well aware" of what he was setting in motion. "Let the chips fall where they may," he declared. His charges afforded a convenient excuse for his failure to unveil his much-heralded action-program, which, despite its ringing preamble, was not a program at all; for the most part, it was merely an elaborate restatement of the views he had been uttering for months.

Malcolm said that the bomb-throwers were so familiar with the layout of his home that he was "quite certain" they knew where each member of his family usually slept. But in his zeal to deny that he had set fire to his home, he blundered and claimed that he had known absolutely "nothing" about the eviction proceedings until he had heard over the radio that Judge Wahl had refused to grant him another extension.

Malcolm pulled out all the stops. He characterized the Nation of Islam as a "criminal organization" and described Elijah Muhammad as a senile old man interested in nothing but money and sex. He also depicted the Messenger, as well as Martin Luther King, as men who placed innocent children in the line of fire. He told his Harlem followers that he had neither compassion for such people nor desire to forgive them. "If anybody can find where I bombed my house," he said, "they can put a rifle bullet through my head.". . .

PROPHECIES

It had become apparent that the political Malcolm, like the youthful criminal Malcolm, was provoking the very retaliation he dreaded. A case in point was his disclosure of Elijah Muhammad's secret contacts with the Ku Klux Klan. The disclosure (which was reminiscent of the way James Eason had disclosed Marcus Garvey's contacts with the Klan) focused on a 1961 meeting Malcolm had held on the Messenger's behalf with representatives of the Klan. Since the K.K.K. opposed racial mixing, Elijah had requested the meeting to enlist its aid in obtaining land that the Nation of Islam could use to implement its separatist doctrines. The Imperial Wizard, the Klan's top leader, had reportedly instructed his subordinates to talk with Elijah's representatives in hope of eliciting information that could be turned over to the federal government.

At the meeting, which was held in Atlanta, Malcolm told the Klan officials what they wanted to hear. Both their movement and his, he asserted, needed to fight the Catholics and the Jews. He asserted that Jews were running the civil rights movement and manipulating its black members. According to an F.B.I. informant who reported the results of the meeting to the Bureau, Malcolm said he could not understand why the Klan allowed Martin Luther King, Jr. to live.

Malcolm also disclosed that Elijah Muhammad had invited American Nazi Party leader George Lincoln Rockwell, who advocated racial separation, to address the NOI's 1962 national convention, where he was booed before the audience could be induced to allow him to speak.

As a result of his disclosures about the Messenger, Malcolm's youthful premonitions about death had become self-fulfilling prophecies. "Surely man is the most ardent contributor to his own doom," he had written years earlier:

> ... Man is actually the tool of his own destruction, ... laboring towards the completion of his own end.

When a *New York Times* reporter asked him why he expected to be killed, he replied, "Because I'm me." ...

The day before the Sunday, February 21 rally that Malcolm had scheduled at the Audubon Ballroom, he checked into the New York Hilton and had supper in the hotel's dining room. By coincidence, Judge Wahl was also there. He was struck by Malcolm's confident demeanor, which was so different from the way he had behaved during the trial.

But that evening when he met his aides, there were tears in his eyes. They were not the only tears he had shed that week; during a meeting with [his sister] Ella, who had agreed to help him purchase a home, tears streamed down his face. It was the first time that Ella had seen him cry since Aunt Sassie's death. "I looked at his eyes," she later recalled. "They seemed blue."

Around ten that evening, a man named Talmadge Hayer, who later testified that he had been offered an undisclosed sum of money to assassinate Malcolm, materialized in the Hilton lobby with two companions and began asking bellmen what room he was in.

Hayer, alias Thomas Hagan, had been a member of the Nation of Islam's Newark, New Jersey, temple for some time. ...

The New York police department's "Bureau of Special Services" (BOSS) knew that an attempt to assassinate Malcolm was imminent. Police spokesmen later emphasized that officials had repeatedly offered him round-the-clock protection.

At least three of the offers had been made in the presence of witnesses.

But the police knew that Malcolm would likely refuse the offers. He was frank about his reluctance to accept protection. A man who had made his reputation defying the authorities could hardly acknowledge that he needed their help. . . .

Moreover, Malcolm, who had had so many run-ins with the police, didn't trust them. (The officers assigned to protect him were probably reporting his activities to their superiors.) "The police know I'm going to be dead by Tuesday," he told a friend. He told another that he had been marked for death by February 21.

Malcolm said police protection wouldn't work:

Nobody can protect you from a Muslim but a Muslim—or someone trained in Muslim tactics.

But the fact that the police could not guarantee his life was not a convincing reason for stopping them from trying.

Malcolm's refusal to request police protection did not excuse New York City's failure to provide it. When he visited Chicago and Philadelphia, policemen stayed with him wherever he went. Malcolm, who hadn't requested their presence, thanked his protectors, just as he did when his own men guarded him. It might have been costly for the New York police to provide the security he needed for weeks or months at a time. However, they could have done it. But even though BOSS officials knew that Malcolm's life was in grave jeopardy, the police department declined to act unless he formally accepted its offer of protection. His refusal to do so took the police "off the hook," one official later asserted cavalierly. . . .

MALCOLM'S LAST DAY

Malcolm arrived at the Audubon at around two. "I don't feel right about this meeting," he told his associate Earl Grant. "I feel that I should not be here. Something is wrong." Grant asked him to cancel the meeting or let someone else speak in his place. Malcolm said he'd think about it.

Wearily, he trudged down one aisle of the sixty-yard-long auditorium to an anteroom adjoining the stage. Usually his presence lit the place. But not that afternoon. He looked like an old man. . . .

It took enormous courage for Malcolm to venture out onto that auditorium stage feeling the way he did. As he stood alone before the audience, the applause became a standing ovation, then subsided. He greeted his listeners, "As salaam alaikum." Enthusiastically, they responded, "Wa alaikum as salaam."

Suddenly, a disturbance occurred in the audience. . . . Two men who were later identified, correctly or otherwise, as Talmadge Hayer and Norman 3X Butler stood and began to argue. "Get your hand out of my pocket," one of them said. The guards who had been posted in front of the stage, near the speaker's rostrum, moved toward the two men, leaving Malcolm unprotected. As they did, a smoke bomb, a home-made device consisting of a lighter-fluid-soaked sock stuffed with matches and combustible film, was detonated. Once again, the audience's attention was diverted.

The shotgun was apparently hidden beneath the jacket of the Black Muslim gunman who was later identified, accurately or otherwise, as Thomas 15X Johnson. The stock of the gun had been shortened and both barrels had been sawed down from thirty inches to eight and a half.

The first barrel was fired at near-point-blank range. Shotgun pellets perforated Malcolm's chest, forming a pattern seven inches high and seven inches across.

Malcolm's hand clutched his chest; blood appeared on his shirt. His lean frame stiffened as he toppled over backward into two of the empty guest chairs. His head struck the stage with a thud.

The man with the shotgun took no chances and fired the second barrel. Simultaneously, Hayer and another pistol-wielding gunman charged the stage and began emptying their guns into Malcolm's motionless body. Members of the shrieking audience threw themselves on the floor to avoid the fusillade.

The three assassins—Hayer later said there were more—tried to escape. One apparently ducked into the women's lounge, from which there were two exits to the street. Hayer and his pistol-packing partner sprinted toward the stairway leading to the main exit, hurdling chairs and firing wildly at the pursuing mob. His confederate was felled by a body block that sent him spinning down the staircase. Hayer was floored by a chair hurled by a man named Gene Roberts, whose suitcoat had been nicked by one of Hayer's bullets. Hayer got up and began limping. Then Reuben Francis [one of Malcolm's bodyguards] shot him in the thigh. Hayer fell face down, rolled over on his back, and tried to shoot back, but his gun failed to fire. Somehow, he regained his footing, made it to the doorway, and started downstairs—half-hopping, half-sliding down the banister. He vaulted over the gunman who had been knocked down the stairs. The latter melted into the pack, which clawed at Hayer, who dropped his .45. The howling mob finally caught him. It would have dispatched him then and there had he not been rescued by the policeman who had been summoned by one of the two officers in the Rose Room.

Possible Government Involvement

George Breitman

Peter Goldman's theory that Malcolm X was slain by Black Muslims has dissatisfied more than one scholar of Malcolm's story. The major problem seems to be that Goldman's recounting comes only from the side of the white police involved in the case. The greater truth was that the police themselves were one of the most-suspected organizations involved in the whole affair. According to George Breitman, the authorities had at least as much motive as anyone in the Nation of Islam for eliminating Malcolm X. Goldman dismissed the possibility of police involvement, calling it an overnourished "conspiracy theory." However, Goldman's view raised a great deal of controversy among black Americans who, like Malcolm, had little faith in the white police and the government of the time. George Breitman is among that group of disbelievers, and offers a compelling argument to contradict Goldman. Breitman has edited books on multiple historical subjects, including fascism in Germany and black nationalism. He is an editor/cowriter of several books on Malcolm X.

A large part of Peter Goldman's book is devoted to the assassination of Malcolm X in February 1965, the ensuing police investigation, and the trial where three men were convicted of the crime in 1966. Here these subjects get the most extensive treatment they have had in any book to date.

Unfortunately, Goldman is hobbled by a thesis he is determined to prove: he did not believe when he began his inquiries, and he does not believe today, that the U.S. government had or could have had any hand in the assassination.

George Breitman, "A Liberal Supports the Government Version," *The Assassination of Malcolm X*, by George Breitman, Herman Porter, and Baxter Smith. New York: Pathfinder Press, 1991. Copyright © 1991 by Pathfinder Press. Reproduced by permission.

He finds the government and its police not guilty, and he accepts their version that Malcolm was killed by three members of the Nation of Islam, at the instigation of unnamed officials of the Nation (although he admits that the prosecution's version of the events as presented in the court was somewhat "tidied up").

"My inquiry," he tells us, "was limited by my own resources, and no doubt also by my color, class, politics, and a certain irremediable skepticism about conspiratorialist explanations of events where nonconspiratorialist explanations appear to be adequate." The factors that reinforced his "skepticism" were undoubtedly his middle-class outlook and the liberal politics that flow so naturally from it.

GOLDMAN'S BIAS

Goldman simply can't believe that the government would do such a thing as participate in the murder of Malcolm. Granted that the government didn't like him, and granted that it gets dangerous people out of the way; it does this, however, he says, "not by some conspiratorial grand design and not ordinarily by murdering them" but through "the far more common sanctions" of "prison and/or exile."

This expression of faith in the nonmurderous character of the government is very touching, and explains a lot about Goldman. But it doesn't prove anything. The government usually resorts to frame-up and prison, but it isn't restricted to them. Not long before Malcolm's death the government approved the assassination of Ngo Dinh Diem, president of South Vietnam. Was Malcolm's life more sacred in the government's eyes than Diem's? All that need be said on this subject is that while assassination is not the government's normal method of repression, it *is* one of its methods. Excluding this possibility is not a promising way to begin an investigation of Malcolm's assassination.

While Goldman merely exonerates the federal government, he positively glows with admiration for the police and prosecutors who prepared the case for trial. Some of them gave him interviews for this book, and they emerge as salt of the earth. Oh, a little cynical perhaps, a little too inclined to cut corners, but otherwise splendid chaps: dedicated to the cause of justice ("Hardly anybody slept at all the first two or three nights, and after that you napped at the squad or Manhattan North when you could and got home long enough to shower and change clothes and just miss seeing the kids off to school"), hard-working (Detective Keeley "worked sixteen hours a day, seven days a week for seven straight weeks before he got his first day off"), generous to the point of self-sacrifice (Goldman thinks they pay with cash out of their own pockets for tips from informers, his evidence being one detective who told him, "I put out maybe a thousand dollars for stoolies [in the Malcolm investigation]. A case like that can put you in the poorhouse.").

All in all, Goldman says, "they conducted a conscientious investigation under extraordinarily difficult circumstances." But at most his book shows why the jury voted to convict the three men indicted by the government, and even that isn't done with complete adequacy.

THE TRIAL

The prosecution had many advantages at the trial—plentiful funds and personnel to work up and "tidy up" a case. Its legal power enabled it to threaten witnesses with arrest if they did not "cooperate." Goldman indicates the police may have threatened Malcolm's associates with arrest in connection with the fire bombing of Harlem Mosque No. 7 shortly after the assassination: "An arson charge can serve you better as a persuader—a legal blunt instrument that can get people talking and doesn't leave any marks." The police actually did imprison the chief prosecution witness for almost a year before the trial, dropping charges against him after he cooperated at the trial. They also benefited strongly from the then widespread prejudice against the Black Muslims.

But the chief advantage the prosecution had was the defense counsel's incompetence and unwillingness to fight. This was particularly true of the four lawyers for the two Black Muslim defendants, Norman 3X Butler and Thomas 15X Johnson. To show that they lacked "the cash for a wide-ranging investigation," Goldman mentions that these four were "court-appointed at the statutory fee of $2,000 per man." But he misses the main point of the fact he cites.

In New York, as in most big cities, court appointment jobs are viewed by all concerned as political plums, despite the relatively low fee. They are given to reliable people, that is, people who do not rock the boat. They don't get such plums from the dominant political machine by trying to prove in court, for example, that the government and police are in collusion in an assassination; if they do that once, they do it knowing they'll never get such an appointment again.

That was why these court-appointed lawyers had to cook up the theory, accepted by hardly anyone but the Black Muslims . . . that Malcolm had been killed by disgruntled members of his own organization. That was why these lawyers did such a poor job in cross-examining the well-coached witnesses for the prosecution. That—and not the compelling logic of the prosecution's case—was basically why the jury voted to convict Butler, Johnson, and Talmadge Hayer. (Hayer had confessed his own part in the murder but wouldn't name his accomplices. He did say, however, that they were not Butler and Johnson.)

So Goldman's "skepticism" spares the defense counsel as well as the government and the police. It is reserved almost exclusively for the "true disbelievers," those who reject the government's version and suspect the government and the police were involved in the murder conspiracy. He lumps together all who will not accept the government version; in his opinion they are all irrational or dishonest. . . .

CREDIBLE EVIDENCE?

On the night of the assassination, the three New York morning papers all reported that two suspects had been arrested at the Audubon Ballroom; Talmadge Hayer by two cops in a scout car that happened accidentally to be passing by, and an unnamed person by Patrolman Thomas Hoy, the only policeman stationed outside the Audubon at the time of the killing. The second editions of these same papers all changed their stories, stating only that Hayer had been captured and not even mentioning the second man. In fact, they never mentioned him again.

Thinking that to be an unusual journalistic procedure, I asked publicly for an explanation. To my knowledge none was ever given in print before Goldman's book. The prosecution's version at the trial, of course, was that only one man had been arrested at the Audubon—Hayer. But it did not call Patrolman Hoy as a witness (neither did the defense).

Now Goldman tells us that it was all a journalistic mix-up—that the man Hoy caught was the same one that the other two cops took into custody. He does not provide details, although his book has room for much trivia, and he does not explain why none of the newspapers bothered to make an explicit correction at the time. But even so, Goldman's version is not unreasonable: it could have happened the way he says. Granting that, however, is not the same as granting that the "second suspect" is "the major single piece of 'evidence' of a state conspiracy."

Twelve days before his assassination Malcolm flew to Paris to speak at a meeting, as he had done three months before without incident. This time he was barred from the country as "undesirable." The French government's explanation was that Malcolm's speech could have "provoked demonstrations that would trouble the public order." After the assassination Malcolm's friends in Paris charged that the French government really had barred him because it thought he would be assassinated on French soil and did not want to bear the onus for such a scandal.

Calling it an unverified rumor, I reported this charge in the *Militant* and asked the press to check it out. If the charge was true, I said, it was important to know why the French government expected a murder attempt, from whom it expected one, and where it got its information. One thing was

Supporters comforted Malcolm as he lay mortally wounded after being shot while speaking at the Audubon Ballroom in New York on February 21, 1965.

certain—the Black Muslims did not have the resources to organize an assassination in France.

Goldman rejects the implications from that fact, which pointed to possible CIA complicity. "A more credible version," he writes, "was that the French acted on the representation of two of their lately liberated colonies, Senegal and the Ivory Coast, that Malcolm—aided and abetted by Nasser and Nkrumah—might try to overthrow moderate, pro-Western governments like their own." Goldman can only deplore the French government's "lack of official candor" and the "tact that forbade anyone's saying so [about Senegal and the Ivory Coast] at the time" because these things have "nourished the conspiratorialist theory of Malcolm's assassination ever since. . . ."

This version is not only more credible (to Goldman) but later he elevates it a little and calls it "most probable." For evidence, he tells us that his account "is based on unpublished reporting in *Newsweek's* files." But we aren't told who did the reporting, where the reporters got their information, and why (besides "tact") the reporting was not published.

Gullible people may accept this kind of stuff, but others will say it's no more convincing than the kind of evidence Goldman rejects as flimsy when advanced by "conspiratorialists." On the face of it, Goldman's version is no more credible than the one put forward by Malcolm's friends in Paris. He has merely suggested another possibility. When I do that, and my possibility points toward the government, that's conspiratorialist; when he does it, and his possibility points away from the government, it's objective reporting, or something of that sort.

I wrote in 1965 that I did not know if Butler and Johnson had any connection with the assassination but strongly doubted they had themselves been present in the Audubon. They were Black Muslims well known to Malcolm's people and therefore could expect to be stopped at the door, questioned, and probably searched by the guards if they had tried to enter the meeting hall.

At the trial the prosecution produced witnesses who swore they saw Butler and Johnson present and shooting at Malcolm. But knowing how the prosecution obtained such testimony and reading of the many contradictions in that testimony leaves me still dubious. It is not impossible that they were present, but to believe it I would have to see or hear some evidence that *they* thought they would be admitted, and a theory explaining *why* they thought so.

This is one of several questions we raised before the trial that were not answered satisfactorily at the trial and that Goldman concedes are still unanswered or troubling today. But they don't trouble him enough to affect his final verdict. When he mentions them, it's proof of his open-mindedness and objectivity. When we mention them, it's proof of paranoia, distortion, etc.

To summarize: Goldman scores a few points, suggests new possibilites on some, and misses the mark altogether on others. That he fails in his main objective I shall now try to show by presenting a "scenario" of the assassination that is not in contradiction with any of the facts reported in his book.

ALTERNATE ASSASSINATION SCENARIO

Around a month before the assassination the police learned of a plot to kill Malcolm. (That's what they said.) How they learned they never said. It could be they learned about it because one or more agents of the conspiracy were members of the police. (It is known that they had infiltrated agents into the Nation of Islam, Malcolm's organizations, and other militant groups. One of these, Gene Roberts, became part of the top Organization of Afro-American Unity (OAAU) leadership, it was revealed in 1970 at the New York Black Panther trial.)

The Bureau of Special Services (BOSS), which was the name of the New York secret police agency at the time, must have communicated this information to Washington, that is, the CIA, because the CIA's keen interest in Malcolm was publicly known. We can assume that the CIA was consulted on and approved, if it did not suggest, the policy then pursued by the BOSS officials, which was to offer Malcolm police protection after having concluded he would have to reject it for political reasons. When Malcolm or a lieutenant did refuse, the man from BOSS told Goldman, "as far as I was concerned, that took us off the hook."

Talmadge Hayer, it is safe to assume, was a member of the murder gang. Whether some or all of the other members were Black Muslims, or ex-Black Muslims, we cannot say, but in this context that question is not decisive. The important thing was that at some point it was decided to proceed with the Malcolm killing. The BOSS agent or agents, assuming for the sake of argument that they were involved, might have taken the initiative in this decision; at the least they would have supported it and made themselves useful in obtaining weapons, devising tactics, raising morale, and encouraging the project in other ways. . . .

The CIA/BOSS officials did not try to break up the murder gang. On the contrary, they told their agent(s) to proceed with business as usual, that is, to help the plot develop. The agent(s) provided the weapons and—more important—inside information (from BOSS agents in the OAAU) about the OAAU and its security methods, and an assassination plan in accord with that information that offered a good possibility that all of the killers could escape after the murder. (They all did, except Hayer, who might well have gotten away too if one of Malcolm's guards had not shot him in the leg.)

The CIA/BOSS officials did not have to organize a murder gang from scratch and in their own name—they found one ready-made. This was an advantage because the participants (except for the agent or agents) wouldn't even know whose interests they were serving. (In this case, the full story may not be disclosed even if Talmadge Hayer decides to talk.) The CIA/BOSS officials did not have to give the order, "Kill Malcolm." All they had to do was let their agents proceed as usual, and wait for the bloody outcome. They were "off the hook" after their offer of police protection was rejected. But that particular assassination might have been stopped if they had tried to stop it, and therefore they were just as guilty of the assassination as the men who pulled the triggers.

PLAUSIBILITY

This "scenario" explains many things that are otherwise inexplicable: why the killers were so audacious, why seventeen of the twenty cops in the special detail assigned to the Audubon were so far from the scene of the crime, why the government felt no qualms about prosecuting Hayer once he was caught at the scene, why it did not produce any BOSS agents as witnesses at the trial, and why it did not produce the Malcolm guard charged with shooting Hayer. It may also help explain why the police publicly accused Malcolm of having fire bombed his own home when his family was asleep in it a week before the assassination. And it definitely disposes of many objections like the so-called "clincher": *Can you imagine the CIA hiring somebody like Hayer?*—because Hayer didn't have to be paid by the CIA to do what the CIA wanted done.

So the argument pointing to the CIA and the police is much more plausible than Goldman makes it out to be in his book, even if his explanation about the second suspect is accepted. Goldman knows that the cops sat back and did nothing to prevent the assassination; in fact, he criticizes them several times for precisely this. What he does not do, what he does not dare to do, is to think through *why* they sat back and to consider how those reasons tie up with both the facts and possibilities in this case. In that sense his book is irresponsible: its effect is to lessen the chances of uncovering the whole truth.

The Link to Louis Farrakhan

Karl Evanzz

Because both the U.S. government and the Nation of Islam watched Malcolm's rise and fall with a close eye, it seems reasonable that Malcolm's death was not just a simple lashing-out by a man on the street. Several scholars have suggested that Malcolm's death was a very complex affair, a plot conceived and executed not just by one or even a small group of men, but by several people, including leaders who were in the public eye at the time. Karl Evanzz has created an elaborate theory about the death of Malcolm X, involving not just Talmadge Hayer, but the FBI, the CIA, and leaders of the Nation of Islam itself. In the following excerpts from his book *The Judas Factor*, he discusses the possibility that Louis Farrakhan, the Nation of Islam member who was once Malcolm's pupil, had a hand in Malcolm's murder. Perhaps Farrakhan, later to become the Nation's highest leader, stood to gain from Malcolm's absence, especially with Elijah Muhammad under scrutiny. In addition to *The Judas Factor*, Evanzz also wrote a book on Muhammad entitled *The Messenger*, published in 1999.

On February 22, someone broke into the Organization of Afro-American Unity (OAAU) office and ransacked it, perhaps in a search for the list of five names that Malcolm X had made of who might assassinate him.

On March 12, the law offices of his attorney, Manhattan Borough President Percy Sutton, were also vandalized. The vandals rifled through files containing copies of papers from lawsuits Sutton had lodged on Malcolm X's behalf. Some of the papers were missing.

Karl Evanzz, *The Judas Factor: The Plot to Kill Malcolm X*. New York: Thunder's Mouth Press, 1992. Copyright © 1992 by Thunder's Mouth Press. Reproduced by permission.

It must be noted that at the time of the break-in, the FBI routinely approved "black bag jobs," the Bureau's term for burglaries.

"Minister Malcolm X did not give to me or, as far as I know, to the police, any names of people who he thought might attempt to assassinate him," Sutton replied when asked whether he had seen the list. Because of what he perceived as their close relationship, Sutton added that he believed that "had there been such names, he would have shared them with me."

Although [Malcolm's wife] Betty Shabazz didn't share her knowledge of the note with Sutton, she did reveal it to freelance photographer Gordon Parks, director of the phenomenally successful movie, *The Learning Tree*, based upon his childhood in the South.

Late on the evening of Malcolm X's assassination, Parks stopped by to see Mrs. Shabazz and her frightened, bewildered little girls. "Is Daddy coming back after his speech, Momma?" asked six-year-old Attalah. Betty Shabazz comforted her but said nothing.

Before Parks departed, Malcolm X's widow showed him the bloodstained list of probable assassins. He copied them down, thinking that he might reveal them in a retrospective for *Life* magazine on his long friendship with the martyr. Unfortunately, neither he nor Betty Shabazz has revealed them to date. On February 23, Richard Helms [an officer of the State Department] sent a final routine memorandum to [a colleague of his] Read at the State Department regarding Malcolm X. The cover page was brief and to the point:

> Pursuant to your recent request, the attached memorandum is furnished to you. The same information is being furnished separately to the Federal Bureau of Investigation.

The nature of the request isn't spelled out in the declassified memorandum, but in view of Read's earlier request for the CIA's Clandestine Services Division to take action against Malcolm X since he was akin to a "foreign agent," one wonders what the memo meant. . . .

SUSPECTS

The trial of the assassins in February, 1966, was pretty much what one would expect for a choreographed political assassination. There were untrustworthy witnesses and contradictory testimony. But there were several noteworthy events. Before the grand jury, [Nation of Islam member] Charles Black-well testified that he had given the German Lugar [pistol] used in the assassination to Gene Roberts, the undercover Bureau of Special Services (BOSSI) agent. He changed his testimony during the trial. The most interesting aspect of the trial was a series of questions posed by prosecutor Vincent J. Dermody. Dermody had uncovered a witness who swore that he saw [suspects Talmadge] Hayer and John Ali together at the Americana Hotel on the night before the assassination. Hayer never answered the question directly, and Dermody mysteriously dropped the line of questioning.

It turned out that the witness who told Dermody that he had seen Hayer and John Ali together at the Americana Hotel on February 20, the night the plot to kill Malcolm X allegedly underwent final rehearsal, was arrested shortly before the trial began. Dermody apparently felt the arrest would reflect poorly on the witness' credibility, so he failed to call him.

Several FBI agents, for reasons which remain unclear, contacted sources in the Boston mosque on February 21 to determine the whereabouts of Louis X Farrakhan. Farrakhan, the FBI noted, "did not appear at the Boston Temple at the Sunday afternoon services . . . no one seems to know where [Louis X Farrakhan] was during that period or, if, in fact, he was actually out of town, but his absence from services was noted."

According to Louis X Farrakhan, he was at the Newark mosque when Malcolm X was assassinated. It seems bizarre that no one in the mosque was aware of his plans to be in Newark.

Oddly enough, the four Black Muslims who Hayer said conspired with him to assassinate Malcolm X—Ben X Thomas (aka Ben Thompson), Leon X Davis, William X, and Wilbur X—were members of the Newark mosque. . . .

DARK EVENTS

In 1968, Louis Lomax received a contract from Twentieth Century Fox to make a movie of the life and death of Malcolm X. According to a script obtained by the FBI, Lomax's central theme was that the U.S. intelligence community played a role in the assassination of Malcolm X. On July 31, 1970, while he was driving to the studio, the brakes on Lomax's car failed, and he crashed and died. . . .

On May 28, 1965, Louis X Farrakhan was transferred from the Boston mosque to New York to serve as head minister of the branches there. In January, 1973, Louis X, who had become the national spokesman for the Nation of Islam, was again making veiled threats against anyone who dared criticize the Messenger [Elijah Muhammad]. The latest was issued after Elijah Muhammad, Louis X, and every other Black Muslim minister received a letter from a man who called himself Hamaas Abdul Khaalis. Khaalis, as it turned out, was Ernest T. 2X McGhee, the former Black Muslim national secretary demoted by Malcolm X in favor of John Ali in 1958. After leaving the Nation of Islam, Khaalis had formed an orthodox Islamic sect known as the Hanafi. The sect's headquarters was located in a home on 16th Street, NW in Washington, D.C., which had been purchased by basketball star Lew Alcindor, who had joined the sect and been renamed Kareem Abdul-Jabbar by Khaalis. Dated January 5, the scathing three-page letter to Muhammad denounced him as a "lying deceiver" as well as questioned the character of Nation of Islam (NOI) founder Wallace D. Fard. Khaalis even called to question the legitimacy of NOI's basis in the Holy Koran.

On January 17, 1973, an eight-member Black Muslim hit squad from the Philadelphia mosque piled into a 1969 Cadillac and another vehicle and headed for Khaalis' home on 16th Street in Washington, a middle-class community known as the "Gold Coast." At a cheap motel that evening, they made final plans to assassinate Khaalis.

The next morning, a member of the team telephoned Khaalis' home to inquire about purchasing pamphlets written by the Hanafi. He was given directions to the home, and he then promised to stop by the next day. When the hit squad arrived at the 16th Street home, Khaalis was away visiting friends and his wife was out shopping. But Almina Khaalis, the leader's 23-year-old daughter, was there, as were her 25-year-old brother Daud and several small children. After Daud sold two of the strangers some pamphlets, a third man claiming to be a repairman came to the door. While Daud was telling him how to get to the rear entrance, the Black Muslims suddenly assaulted him and forced their way into the house. Within seconds, all eight of the armed Philadelphia Black Muslims were in the home. Daud was taken to a bedroom on the third floor and forced to kneel on a prayer rug. A pillow was placed against his head as one of the gunmen shot him point blank three times.

Almina was dragged upstairs next. "Why did you write those letters?" the assailants asked again and again. Using a shirt to muffle the sound of gunfire, the assassins forced Almina into a closet on the third floor and shot her three times in the head. . . .

Although evidence was left at the scene of the crime, no significant breaks came in the case until Detective Ronald Washington of the District of Columbia Metropolitan Police Department moved temporarily to Philadelphia and infiltrated Mosque No. 12, the mosque the assassins had been linked to. After tracing long distance telephone calls made by the assassins on the day of the murder, detectives honed in on James Price, a member of the hit team. Price, who was already suspected of a homicide in Philadelphia, confessed to the crimes in June, and turned state's witness in July. Based on Price's confessions, the baby killers were soon in custody.

THE ANGER OF LOUIS X

The day before Price was scheduled to testify against his co-conspirators, the same man who had called Malcolm X a hypocrite and who stated in the same breath that hypocrites deserved to die, gave a radio sermon on behalf of Elijah Muhammad. During the radio broadcast, which was reportedly heard by Price, Louis X Farrakhan did not apologize for the dastardly destruction of innocent black babies by Black Muslims, but he did have this to say:

> Let this be a warning to those of you who would be used as an instrument of a wicked government against our rise. Be careful, because when the government is tired of you they're going to dump you back into the laps of your people.
>
> And though Elijah Muhammad is a merciful man and will say, "Come in," and forgive you, yet in the ranks of the black people today there are younger men and women who have no forgiveness in them for traitors and stool pigeons.
>
> And they will execute you, as soon as your identity is known.

After hearing Louis X Farrakhan's radio broadcast, Price refused to testify. The next day, he was found hanged in his jail cell.

Chapter 5

Malcolm's Legacy

Malcolm X

Following Malcolm into Islam

Steven Barboza

The Nation of Islam and the Black Muslim movement would never be as controversial or as closely
watched again after Malcolm X was assassinated.
But the movement didn't die; it lived on in various
forms. Steven Barboza, a member of the Islam faith,
talks here about how he discovered Malcolm's message a decade after Malcolm's death. People like Barboza are living testaments to the fact that the philosophy that Malcolm X represented did not die with
him. There is a legacy that has been passed on to a
new generation of African Americans. Barboza is a
journalist who has written for the *Washington Post*,
the *New York Times*, and *USA Today*. His book *American Jihad: Islam After Malcolm X* provides a unique
look into his own life and the lives of several other
black American Muslims living in what he calls
"Islam country."

I discovered Malcolm X late.

He died in 1965, eight years before I heard his message.
Yet for me his words were fresh and new—and they could
still strike fear into people's hearts.

Many years before Hollywood got around to putting his
life on film, and decades before his X adorned baseball caps,
I would hole myself up in a library and listen to recordings
of his speeches. They were full of pent-up rage. He lashed
out at the white man, whom he called a "blue-eyed devil"
and derided as a liar, a drunkard, an adulterer, a thief, a
murderer. I marveled at his gall, at the convincing tone of his
seditious voice, at the power and conviction with which he
said the black man's "natural religion" was Islam. He said
the American Negroes' ancestors were, in fact, African Mus-

lims and America wanted to hide this from the Negro because this country actually feared what the Negro could bring himself to do if he set his mind to it. Things could get out of hand.

I wanted to know more, so I visited the Nation of Islam's Boston temple, where I attended a sort of Sunday-school class. There, a well-dressed minister inveighed hard against Christianity, calling it the religion of "death" and saying its symbol, the crucifix, provided clear enough proof of that. Just open your eyes and see how Jesus was nailed to the cross, and how Christians adore the whole idea, he said.

On the streets, I met bow-tied brothers hawking bean pies and *Muhammad Speaks*, the Nation's newspaper. They eagerly preached one on one, and their dignified bearing—it seemed drilled into them—appealed to that part of me attracted to uniforms and regimentation. They were sharp, respectful, and streetwise—nationalist soldiers molded into a fearless image, that of Malcolm. . . .

PERSONAL EXPERIENCE

I grew up in New Bedford, Massachusetts, the New England seaport town where my grandparents settled after emigrating from the Cape Verde archipelago off West Africa at the start of this century. I was raised Catholic and for one fleeting moment in the fifth or sixth grade I dreamt of becoming a priest. In retrospect I actually considered this no more seriously than I had considered taking up the clarinet or flute, neither of which I play today. It was a passing thought. But faith itself was not. This wasn't something one ordinarily questioned; it was to be inherited without squabble; it was something one was supposed to take for granted, as one does his own name.

I attended religion classes and received the sacraments but was no more religious for having done so than I was for watching television. Building my faith in God was supposed to have evolved through a simple and neat process, extended over the period of my youth, so long as I routinely showed my face in church. But for me and some of my peers, the church aisle came to symbolize more a runway for modeling Easter outfits than a path to the altar, communion, and God's forgiveness.

My links to the old country, at least, were strong and direct. At home I ate island cuisine and heard Crioulo, an

Africanized Portuguese, and there were plenty of stories about what life back in the old country was like. All of this implied I was somehow different, yet I was confused about my heritage. I failed to see how it fit into the scheme of things vis-à-vis racism in America.

And then I discovered Malcolm X. He summed up much that was ugly about America, eloquently telling off whites.

But his life showed me something eminently more useful than skillful oratory: what role religion could play as one approached this race-conscious society. He provided an example of how a man could use conviction as a powerful instrument to change the course of life—one's own and others'. His remarkable ability to transform himself from hood to cleaned-up spokesman for the Nation of Islam and then to Sunni Islam—that was his real message.

Robert Penn Warren wrote: "Malcolm X was a latter-day example of an old-fashioned type of American celebrated in grammar school readers, commencement addresses, and speeches at Rotary Club lunches—the man who 'makes it,' the man who, from humble origins and with meager education, converts—by will, intelligence, and sterling character—his liabilities into assets. Malcolm X was of that breed of American, autodidacts and homemade successes, that has included Benjamin Franklin, Abraham Lincoln, P.T. Barnum, Thomas Alva Edison, Booker T. Washington, Mark Twain, Henry Ford, and the Wright Brothers."

I was to learn that many other converts had discovered Malcolm too, and had grown beyond the point he had reached in the religion—Malcolm ended his spiritual journey in orthodoxy, where many converts began their own, taking their Islamic studies seriously enough to matriculate at universities in Egypt, Saudi Arabia, and elsewhere. Some Muslim converts, leery of the personality cult that developed around Malcolm's revived image—which inspired a $100 million market in X caps, clothing, and paraphernalia—are quick to point out that Malcolm was Sunni Muslim for a relatively short time, and that most of his talks were made while he followed Elijah Muhammad.

JIHAD

Regardless of whether one remembers the angry Malcolm X of earlier days or the equality conscious El-Hajj Malik El-Shabazz [Malcolm's later name], his stamp on the American

Islamic landscape is enduring, his influence undeniable. Many Muslim converts were steered toward the religion through his autobiography, as told to Alex Haley. Allah, Muslims say, makes Muslims. How He seems to have done this in the United States in many cases was through Malcolm the Instrument.

Muslims still carry out their obligations for *jihad* ("striving"), with Malcolm long gone, and they do so in a nation that misunderstands them and misconstrues their motives.

The Qur'an forbids aggressive warfare. In the Qur'an, Allah prescribes fighting to preserve freedom of religion, dignity, and conscience. *Jihad*, which merely means "striving," or "struggling," is required of Muslims to defend themselves. *Jihad*, however, has been widely interpreted to signify "fighting," its secondary meaning, as in "holy war" waged against enemies of the *ummah*, the greater Muslim community.

Part of the reason is this: Within centuries after the death of the Prophet, Muslim jurists divided the world not into secular and sacred realms, but into realms of belief and unbelief—the House of Peace and the House of War, or Unbelief. All within the dominion of the Islamic state—including *ummahs* of Christians and Jews—were considered integral parts of the federation, the House of Peace. All outside of it carried the distinct possibility of aggression. Peace, then, had to be "waged." And it was.

By the beginning of the eighth century the *jihad* effort dwindled and Muslims lived side by side with non-Muslims, carrying on diplomatic relations and trade. But Muslims' reputation for sword-bearing had taken root.

Actually, there are several kinds of *jihad*: the first is *jihad bil nafs*, which means "striving within the self." This is considered the greatest *jihad*. The second *jihad* is *jihad fi sabil Allah*, "striving in the path of Allah." This *jihad* is carried out by word or deed—by the tongue, by the pen, or as a last resort, by the hand. Allah forbids Muslims to submit passively to the injustices of others. He gives permission to strive against His enemies:

> Permission (to fight in self-defense) is (now) given to those (Muslims) against whom war is waged (for no reason), because they have been done injustice to, and Allah has indeed might and power to help them;

> Those who have been driven out of their homes without any just cause. Their only fault was that they said, "Our Lord is

Allah." If Allah had not repelled some peoples by means of others, cloisters and churches and synagogues and mosques wherein the name of Allah is mentioned very frequently, would have been razed to the ground in large numbers. And Allah will surely help one who helps His cause. Allah is, indeed, All-Powerful, All-Mighty.

Qur'an 22:39–40

Malcolm X's "greater *jihad*" was his striving to turn his life around and mold himself as a Muslim; his "lesser *jihad*" was talking back at white America—which translated as offering blacks a psychological alternative, a perhaps non-pacifist plan for fighting back.

The greater *jihad* is well underway among American converts who seek to transform themselves in the light of Muslim ideals and injunctions in the Qur'an.

Malcolm as Cultural Hero

Molefi Kete Asante

The question of what to do with Malcolm's teachings
is still asked today. Molefi Kete Asante is among
many who believe that the Afrocentric theories of
Malcolm X are key to the future of black American
society. Asante is a prolific scholar at Temple University who has written multiple books on the subject of
Afrocentricity, a philosophy for the restoration of a
sort of historical consciousness for the African
American. Here he discusses the need for strengthening what he calls the "self-confidence" of the
African American. To Asante, a certain amount of independence is needed from the European/white
American, and that road to independence is a "cultural path" that Malcolm started. The end result of
this path, in Asante's view, will be a brand new
African American community.

I have always been concerned with how Malcolm X interacted with his community to create a more revolutionary response to cultural domination. Since culture is a product of
the historical processes which lead to self-conscious recognition of defining characteristics in the social, political, and
economic arenas, Malcolm is the epitome of the great opposition to domination. He was a cultured individual.

As an Afrocentrist I understand culture to be more than a
surplus to material growth because it is fundamental to national self-assertion; indeed, it is the basis of any sustainable
material value. Without culture you cannot hope to keep or
to add to your material value. Our history, if anything, has
always been one in which men and women who have been
deeply committed to equality have borne witness to an intensely collective concept of culture. Malcolm was such a

person. He was pre-eminently a cultural spokesperson, a cultured person, an analyst and theorist of culture, a revolutionary cultural scientist. Thus, when he is examined within the context of his own community and within the framework of the African-American situation, he emerges as a concrete example of the cultural hero. . . .

A NEW CONCEPT OF CULTURE

With the Age of Malcolm a new epoch began in the conception of a national culture or cultural nationalism causing a far-reaching revolution in the traditional views held by members of African-American institutions. Malcolm was not merely "our manhood," as [actor] Ossie Davis nobly put it at Malcolm's funeral, but the keeper of the ancestral flames of a proactive response to the human condition. His own life represented the rebirth of the extensive African-American commitments to cultural reconstruction which are not yet concluded. Despite the various political and social contours of the past twenty years, we have not yet succeeded in wholly realizing the fundamental cultural vision of Malcolm X. . . .

What is necessary is the consistent and persistent dissemination of the ideas Malcolm espoused in regard to culture, essentially a "pattern or the habit of seeing for ourselves, hearing for ourselves, thinking for ourselves, and then we can come to an intelligent judgment for ourselves."

Malcolm saw that the adaptation of our ideas, attitudes, language, and history to the social and cultural imperatives of the African people was the first requirement for a comprehensive transformation. There could be no other interface with our historical destiny; we had to center ourselves in our African reality. . . .

With Malcolm's challenge—that we were Africans—it became clearer that "Negro" was dead. In the struggle of ideas where cultural considerations were seen as primary, that is, fundamental, the old Negro order, hailed in its day [in the 1920s and 1930s] by Alain Locke and others as the "new Negro," was permanently laid to rest by Malcolm. . . . Malcolm brought discontent within the camp of the old order, creating by the power of his logic, schisms in the conservative body politic of African America. It is easy to understand the preeminent position of Malcolm as a cultural figure when in addition to all I have said we consider the intense reaction of the white American establishment to his call for black cultural nationalism. Malcolm was considered an extremist and a militant by most of the white press. Of course, the African-American press, itself often tied to the white corporate structure, was hardly any better on Malcolm.

The cultural epoch of Malcolm, of course, wears a multi-faceted umbrella under which walks a new woman and man born of cultural struggle and understanding [theorist Maulana] Karenga's notion of "history as the struggle and record of humans in the process of humanizing the world, i.e., shaping it in their own image and interests." Even now the legacies we have inherited from Malcolm are the most dominant motifs of our approach to humanity. Since culture involved struggle and struggle developed culture, Malcolm understood the necessity for the African American to recognize value in our traditions.

Malcolm made an end to the apologia of the Negro and declared that we would "be free by any means necessary." While we often understand Malcolm to include self-defense, we know from his teachings that he was committed to changing the way we thought about ourselves and Africa. Planting the seed of an affirming African presence, his cultural project was the root from which we grow strong, vital African sentiments and attitudes. Malcolm's project gave the impulse to the cultural nationalism that exists always just below the emotional surface of every African American. Along with this impulse to cultural nationalism, Malcolm's project encouraged the ethical value of Afrocentric institutions. Thus, the cultural epoch initiated by Malcolm developed very quickly into a thousand parallel universes of freedom which stood against the sacrifice of Africanity to some abstract concept of integration. What Malcolm X strove for was the dispelling of illusions because illusions were not based on African centrality. Culture, to be meaningful, had to be Afrocentric.

THE MEANING OF AFROCENTRIC CULTURE

Reconstructive culture as understood by Malcolm was fostered by social responsibility based on the understanding of history. Such responsibility in the context of the African-American community could only exist on the basis of cultural solidarity. What Malcolm understood was the need for mutual appreciation of Africanity as the first level of overcoming oppression based on physical or mental brutality.

The appreciation of Africanity is the same as self-acceptance. When this prerequisite is absent there is the possibility of . . . extreme misorientation.

Malcolm was a cultural worker in his most elementary manifestation. His aim always was to collect the people into a community of solidarity so that new cultural energies would arise for the common purpose. In the creation of community solidarity he wanted to establish a national consciousness which would render ineffective the old Negro order. His language characterizing that order is well known. Malcolm says, "Also this type of so-called Negro, by being intoxicated over the white man, he never sees beyond the white man. He never sees beyond America. He never looks at himself or where he fits into things on the world stage . . . And it puts him in the role of a beggar—cowardly, humble,

Malcolm X

Uncle Tomming beggar on anything that he says is—that should be his by right."

Malcolm's view of culture was centered principally on an Afrocentric foundation. He did not assert and would never assert the development of the national culture as a result of the economic necessity. He neither tried to prove nor would he have been so inclined to prove that historical events were always caused by economic necessity. In reality, Malcolm was an astute observer of the historical conditions of African Americans and he saw that in the serious reconstruction of African culture, the struggle for power and the ability to create categories which are accepted by others frequently played a much more important role than economic necessity. Beyond this, however, was his insistence on African cultural autonomy by which he meant all things considered cosmological, axiological, epistemological, and aesthetical. Given such autonomy it was possible to imagine a culture of resistance as well as a reconstructive culture. By virtue of its affirming posture this new view of culture became, in Malcolm's theory, a critique of oppressive reality. This critique was presented in Malcolm's rhetoric as a missile against the enemies of the African-American people. Indeed, his language was complete as the expression of the national culture. More so than Langston Hughes in poetry or Martin Luther King, Jr., in civil rights, it was Malcolm who elevated the people's street language to a national style. Few passages in the history of oratory can compare with the straightforward logic and dynamic cadence of Malcolm saying, "So when I come in here to speak to you, I'm not in here speaking as a Baptist or a Methodist or a Democrat or a Republican or a Christian or a Jew or—not even as an American. Because if I stand up here—if I could stand up here and speak to you as an American we wouldn't have anything to talk about. The problem would be solved. So we don't even profess to speak as an American. We are speaking as—I am speaking as a Black man." Indeed, one might argue that Malcolm's ground of contact with the people was so vast and that his groundedness with the masses so profoundly human that he earned the title "spokesman" in a manner wholly unlike any other African-American leader. He was not spokesman by virtue of his official status within the African-American community but spokesman because he actually spoke what was in our hearts the way we would have spoken it if we had been so eloquent. Language is never the invention of individual people but rather the creation of the community as a whole. Culturally, Malcolm tapped the most creative aspect of African-American life, drawing upon the proverbs, the folklore, the nuances, the syntax, and the grammar of the people's creation to make his own discourse. Between his discourse and ours there was hardly any difference; he spoke and when he spoke he took the words right out of our mouths. . . .

CULTURAL CONSCIOUSNESS

Perhaps the principal clue to Malcolm's understanding of culture emerges when he demonstrates his rationale for action: the struggle against the condition of oppression. For us, culture has no other practical end. It must be the regaining of freedom in order to be truly effective as humans in history.

He had arrived at his analysis of the role of culture, by which he meant all of the seven constituents later conceptualized by Maulana Karenga as the Nguzo Saba, through testing the historical choices made by African Americans. The

Civil Rights Movement came under extremely close scrutiny since it had galvanized thousands and had captured the imagination of the black establishment. What Malcolm discerned, however, was the ineffectiveness of a movement which did not address the cultural question. He spent his life asserting this theme and the varied implications of this theme. If some found his theses violent, it was because he laid them down without excuse, and because the system of white domination of African Americans was violent. What more could he do than present a direct challenge to Africans in America to take up arms and march into battle? How else does one approach a sustained physical and psychological assault? What else is real? Thus, Malcolm had gained his own sanity and was located in an Afrocentric mode before he broke with the teachings of Elijah Muhammad, teachings that had been a major bulwark against the indecencies of white Christianity. . . .

Malcolm's cultural consciousness exalted resistance to outrage and became, by virtue of his commitment to the survival of his own culture, a key aspect of his nationalism:

> And the Motto of the Organization of Afro-American Unity is By Any Means Necessary. We don't believe in fighting a battle that's going to—in which the ground rules are to be laid down by those who suppress us. We don't believe that we can win in a battle where the ground rules are laid down by those who exploit us. We don't believe that we can carry on a struggle trying to win the affection of those who for so long have oppressed and exploited us.

On another occasion, Malcolm could ask the African-American community questions like the following: Why should whites be running the stores in the African-American community? Why should whites own all of the businesses in the African-American community?. . .

WHY WE LISTENED

One reason why we listened to him was . . . the virtue of recognition. Malcolm resembled us at our best, in our most authoritative manner, in our humanity, in our style, in our humor, in our secrets, and in the manner of our treatment of each other. In these things collectively, and with specific qualities, we each could individually admire Malcolm's life as a testament to African-American culture.

While we must admit that Malcolm resembled us in our highest cultural reality, he was also our cultural teacher.

Creating a curriculum of culture from our own history he elevated the art of instruction by serving as the model for what he taught. If he taught us that courage was more rewarding than cowardice, he demonstrated by his own life that he believed what he taught. If the government was full of "tricksters," then African-American leaders should not have coffee with the tricksters. He met the protectors and defenders of the establishment only to tell them of the grievances we rightly held. Thus, culture, for Malcolm, was proactive and he promulgated the view that "by any means necessary" we had to advance from the oppressed state in which we found ourselves in America. The broad dissemination of this message alone was sufficient to create for him a place in our cultural history because no one had ever taught quite so effectively, or so directly.

Malcolm's cultural path will not be complete until it is fully realized in the active political and social lives of African Americans. In the end, that is the only authentic test for his conception of an Afrocentric culture. He becomes a figure transformed in the actuality of our own historical experiences, thus, to live Malcolm, as some African Americans in Philadelphia and other places have begun to do. . . is only one aspect of culture. He is represented by a string of solid black beads. However, the reality of Malcolm at this level does and cannot replace the need for authentic confrontation at another level with oppression, menticide, self-hatred, and exploitation. We can only go forward from here with the aim of fulfilling the Malcolmian project of removing African self-hatred and restoring African self confidence.

The Nation of Islam and Racial Separation

Roy L. Brooks

In his book *Integration or Separation?* Roy L. Brooks offers some potential drawbacks of the separation of whites and blacks under the teachings of Malcolm X and the Black Muslims. Brooks is a writer for the Harvard University Press who produces books with a debate focus. Like many of his works, *Integration or Separation?* presents both the advantages and disadvantages of each side of the issue. The following excerpt from the book provides a background for the decline of the Nation of Islam after Malcolm, and a summary of what made their separatist strategy both effective and flawed.

Religious faith and stringent private and public codes of morality served as a foundation for launching the Black Muslims' social reform movement in the late 1950s. Significantly, the change in emphasis coincided with Malcolm X's ascendancy within the Nation. Elijah Muhammad seemingly recognized the appeal of the handsome, articulate Malcolm X. As he told his older ministers, "You are teaching the same thing we taught in the thirties. Malcolm X is modern times: he knows how to help me." And soon enough Malcolm X emerged as the most influential voice of the Nation of Islam. . . .

TOTAL SEPARATION

In the 1950s Malcolm X started a newspaper, *Muhammad Speaks,* to help disseminate the Muslim message. By 1959 the Muslims were able to tap into the mainstream American media. The charismatic Malcolm X appeared on a nationally televised special news program in that year, "The Hate That Hate Produced." The appearance led to many speaking en-

Roy L. Brooks, *Integration or Separation?* Cambridge, MA: Harvard University Press, 1996. Copyright © 1996 by the President and Fellows of Harvard College. Reproduced by permission.

gagements and considerable coverage in popular periodicals. As one commentator writes, "the white press . . . made [Malcolm X] famous, and notoriety sharply enhanced his attraction to the masses."

While the teachings of Fard Muhammad laid the blueprint for political and social change, Elijah Muhammad and Malcolm X formulated the particulars of the program. At the heart of the plan rested the decision that Black Muslims would not patiently and passively wait for Armageddon. Malcolm X, in particular, with a fiery rhetoric and a confrontational style, urged immediate and sweeping changes for African Americans. Given that whites are inherently evil, African Americans must "get away from the devil as soon and as fast as [they] can." Simply put, the program they devised called for African Americans to reject every aspect of white America—in essence, to isolate themselves from whites, so that they could remain pure.

Elijah Muhammad and Malcolm X believed total separation was the simplest way to repudiate white society in its entirety. They viewed integration as a scheme by white people to save themselves from damnation. Furthermore, they argued, white people did not propose integration when they were the undisputed rulers of the world. It was only after they saw the impending destruction of their empire and the loosening of their hold over the African Americans that they began to consider integration. Muhammad also maintained that African Americans would not improve their lives through integration, because whites would not allow integration to advance to the point where it would disadvantage them. Through it all, the "So-Called Negro" would continue to remain at the bottom of American society. Hence the solution for African Americans is total separation.

Elijah outlined the essential requirements for total separation in speeches across the country as well as in two documents entitled "What Do Muslims Want?" and "Message to the Blackman in America." The simplistic "What Do Muslims Want?" sets forth ten points:

1. Full, complete freedom
2. Equal justice under the law, regardless of creed, class, or color
3. Equality of opportunity
4. A separate state or territory—either on this continent or elsewhere

5. Release of all believers of Islam held in federal prisons
6. An immediate end to police brutality and mob attacks against African Americans
7. Equal employment opportunities
8. Exemption from all taxation
9. Equal education, including separate schools
10. Intermarriage or race mixing should be prohibited. The religion of Islam should be taught without hindrance or suppression

In "Message to the Blackman in America," Muhammad declares that African Americans must separate themselves from whites in all ways—mentally, economically, and physically. Mental separation occurs when African Americans repudiate the heritage and culture of the "slavemaster" and adopt their own, that of a racially superior tribe of Shabazz. Economic separation includes living frugally, as debt is bondage to whites, and supporting only African American (that is, Muslim-owned) businesses. Physical separation, of course, is the ultimate goal, which will occur when African Americans settle in their own territory in North America or elsewhere. All of Elijah Muhammad's major writings express similar ideas, and the gist of his thinking is that a successful program of liberation must touch every aspect of the African American's life.

SEPARATIST STRATEGIES

The Black Muslim program appears to contain three alternative scenarios. The first and least complex is complete separation of the races. Black Muslims claim that because black identity is unique and integration is hypocritical, African Americans have no place in the white American system. Malcolm X maintained that the "only solution was complete separation," and Elijah Muhammad declared that "our former slavemasters are obligated to maintain and supply our needs in the separate territory for the next 20 to 25 years—until we are able to produce and supply our own needs." Total separation was also viewed as a form of reparations for the "400 years of free labor" white Americans had taken from African Americans. Muslims demanded separate land in which the Nation could set up its own system, complete with farms, factories, businesses, schools, and its own set of laws. Four or five southern states would suffice for a viable nation that enjoyed total self-reliance and self-sufficiency. Muhammad preferred to remain in the United States rather than return to Africa, because "we have as much right to the soil as the white man. Why should we claim the land of our Black brothers in Africa; our destiny is right here in America."

In the second alternative, if total separation were untenable, the Muslim program called for separation within the confines of white society. Black Muslims accept this imperfect form of racial separation because they believe "separation . . . can . . . take a psychological, a religious and an economic form even if it cannot express itself in the ultimate guise of a national territory." The Nation is willing to settle for a "nation within a nation," but only if whites make certain concessions. First, they must establish separate schools staffed by African Americans, because whites do not teach "the truth." In addition, Muslims want freedom from taxation and a law forbidding racial mixing. Nor do they want to participate in white people's wars or be considered United States citizens. In essence, Black Muslims want to be isolated as much as possible while living within the white society. They want to practice their religion in peace and prosper economically without white interference. In return, Muslims would continue to obey the laws and respect the citizens of the United States.

Because this proposal too was premised on tremendous governmental cooperation, which was not forthcoming, Muhammad fashioned a separatist strategy that required no governmental intervention. It called for the creation of African American educational and economic institutions within the African American community. In response, Black Muslims did establish their own private schools, called the University of Islam, for ages one through nineteen. The Nation also created a five-point economic plan. The plan admonishes African Americans to: (1) recognize the necessity for unity and group operation (activities); (2) pool your resources, physically as well as financially; (3) stop wanton criticism of everything that is black-operated and black-owned; (4) remember, jealousy destroys from within; and (5) work hard in a collective manner. Thus, the movement attempted to build self-reliance through a mixture of economic achievement, black pride, collective thinking, and a strong work ethic.

The Nation of Islam, in short, presented a program of

racial separation replete with demands, details, and alternative strategies, in the event that the United States government would not meet its demands. This multilayered program rested on a racial ideology composed of religious tenets, black pride, self-reliance, and vulgar racism. Supporting the program were thousands of followers and strong leaders, working during the most active period of civil rights since Reconstruction—the 1950s and 1960s. Despite these advantages, the Nation eventually weakened and the movement lost its momentum.

THE DECLINE

In the 1960s the Black Muslim movement had an estimated membership of 100,000 to 250,000. James Baldwin hailed it as the "only grass roots Negro movement in the United States." Indeed, the Nation of Islam was widely considered the most powerful and feared black nationalist movement since Marcus Garvey. At the very least, it was a formidable social-religious movement. The Black Muslims seemed to offer thousands of African Americans a solution to racial oppression. From the mid-1960s, however, the Nation's influence steadily declined. It never produced the social reform it had prophesied.

Conflicting ideologies and fractured leadership were significant factors leading to the Nation's decline. Muslim leaders argued about whether Fard was really Allah and about other tenets of Black Muslim ideology. Muhammad's son, Wallace, questioned his father's teachings on Fard. Malcolm X spoke publicly after President Kennedy's assassination, though he had been ordered not to do so, and angered the vast majority of Americans when he said the killing signified the "chickens were coming home to roost." He was then removed as minister from his temple. Perhaps in retaliation, Malcolm questioned Elijah's morality when two secretaries revealed they had ongoing sexual relations with Elijah Muhammad and had borne his children. Malcolm left the organization and, after a visit to Mecca, formed his own group, the Organization of Afro-American Unity (OAAU). Then, in a sudden reversal of belief, he rejected the idea of building a separate black nation in North America based on racial superiority. Many commentators believe that he totally abandoned the concept of separatism, but it is more likely that his views had just grown more nuanced. His goal was to achieve racial autonomy as a first step in a long struggle toward "independent black nationhood."

Malcolm's departure undoubtedly contributed to the Nation's loss of influence. In addition, its strict rules of behavior could not withstand modern mores. In 1974, toward the end of his life, Elijah Muhammad consented to jettison Black Muslim ideology and adopt the changes favored by his son, Wallace Muhammad. When Elijah died in 1975, Wallace was named as his successor. This shocked many in the Nation because the younger man had been suspended many times for refusing to believe that Fard was Allah. Wallace changed the movement from one advocating separatism and racial superiority to one advocating orthodox Islamic practices, and even allowed whites to become members of the Nation. Feeling betrayed and outraged, a group of Muslims, led by Minister Louis Farrakhan (Louis Eugene Walcott, born in 1933), broke away. Farrakhan's group returned to the Nation's original racist theology and separatist program, with a few modifications. For example, whereas Elijah Muhammad rejected Marcus Garvey's return-to-Africa strategy, Farrakhan saw emigration to Africa as a credible option. And while Elijah Muhammad considered territorial separation within the United States as a form of reparations, Farrakhan expanded the notion of reparations to include not only money but also the release of all African Americans from state and federal penitentiaries. Today, Farrakhan's group is generally regarded as the continuation of the Nation of Islam (Farrakhan considers it to be the "true" Nation) but, although more influential than Wallace's group, it is less powerful than Elijah's Nation was at its height.

One scholar suggests that Elijah Muhammad's movement simply peaked as a social force and could not attract additional recruits because most African Americans did not believe that "going somewhere else" was an acceptable solution to the race problem. Perhaps the Muslims' emphasis on racial pride in the end served to further convince African Americans that they should remain a part of America "without apology for [their] blackness"; that they should stay and fight for their rightful place in American society. Moreover, in the 1960s most African Americans were stirred by the new promise of racial integration. Conversely, the antagonistic and racist rhetoric against whites and the black superiority doctrine surely deterred many potential followers.

Economic failure was another contributing factor to the Nation's decline. Although the movement correctly recognized the link between economic self-sufficiency and socioeconomic power, it was never able to achieve economic self-sufficiency. Most Muslims were unskilled or semiskilled laborers; many were employed by white-owned businesses and were thus dependent on white America. On its own and without resources, the movement was unable to generate the autonomous economic system it had hoped to create. As one commentator has noted: "Membership in the Nation could . . . insulate [individuals] from some of the frustration of living in the white [person's] society; but it could not bring [them] equality, justice, or freedom within the American system."

Finally, despite the Nation's bombastic rhetoric and radical ideas, Elijah Muhammad chose a policy of political nonengagement, a policy that may well have destroyed the momentum the movement had so carefully cultivated. Privately, Malcolm X was convinced that the Black Muslims could have had a significant impact if they engaged in political activism. African Americans in the 1960s were eager to participate in the political process through voting or fielding candidates. In rejecting that path, the Nation cut itself off from a substantial source of potential support. Such passivity created a void that was filled by other black nationalist organizations, such as the Black Panther Party. Similarly, the plans for total separation lay dormant because significant government participation was required to implement them. The leadership knew this, yet it took no action to force the government to consider total separation as a serious alternative to integration. Possibly they refused on principle to strike a deal with the "devil" or to rely upon governmental assistance in any form, but these principles proved self-defeating, as they could not succeed without governmental intervention. Elijah Muhammad chose to wait for the War of Armageddon—a sure sign of procrastination.

In short, internal ideology conflict, the obvious limitations of a "theologically falsified racial doctrine" in a secular age, the African American appetite for racial integration in the 1960s, the lack of an independent economic system, passive political leadership, and the simple fact that territorial separation was "politically unrealizable," all contributed to the decline of the movement.

Pros and Cons

As much a theological as a social movement, the Nation of Islam offers a few valuable lessons for African Americans. The importance of racial pride and unity in uplifting and mobilizing the masses is one of them. Garvey, however, taught this first and with greater drama. Black Muslims also teach us that religion, traditional moral values, and the work ethic can combine to create an effective program of behavior modification, turning career criminals into law-abiding citizens and allowing the poor and downtrodden to help themselves.

The Black Muslim program also has negative features. A plan of racial separation, regardless of what good it does for African American self-esteem, loses the moral high ground as well as practicality when it is grounded in racist ideology or theology. Without creating and executing a political program and without government cooperation, territorial separatists cannot succeed.

Elijah Muhammad nonetheless symbolized unity and pride for African Americans. Rhetoric and racism aside, he showed a true love for African Americans and a genuine concern for their plight. Elijah Muhammad, later Malcolm X, and now Louis Farrakhan have dared to say what most African Americans wanted to say: "We have had enough." Together, these leaders offered a dignified proposal for African Americans, a potential haven from racial discrimination and oppression.

Rethinking Malcolm's Image

Angela Y. Davis

The legacy of Malcolm X can be viewed in many terms besides his general contributions to African American culture. Malcolm's life also had an impact on the lives of both African American youth and black women all over America. In the following selection, Angela Y. Davis argues that Malcolm has been co-opted by young black men of today as a symbol of resistance and male authority. Davis worries that these young people don't seem to understand Malcolm's true philosophy. Unfortunately, a byproduct of this faulty overly masculinized image—which is partly constructed and proliferated by the media—is that women are excluded from utilizing Malcolm's message of resistance. Davis belongs in a camp of writers trying to use Malcolm's legacy to enrich as many different aspects of modern culture, both black and white, male and female, as possible. She writes from her post as professor of the history of consciousness at the University of California in Santa Cruz. During her tenure she has written about women, culture, and politics as a field of study.

In 1992, within a context constructed by ubiquitous images of Malcolm as the *essential Black man*, the juxtaposition of the words "Malcolm" and "feminist" rings strange and oxymoronic. Yet this is precisely why I feel compelled ... to formulate a number of questions regarding some possible feminist implications of his legacy. I will not presume to answer all the questions I pose. Indeed, many of them are speculative in the Socratic sense, designed more to shift the focus of the popular discourse on Malcolm X rather than guide a substantive inquiry into his political history.

MALCOLM AND FEMINISM

The first set of questions: Is it possible that if Malcolm had not been shot down on February 21, 1965, he might be identifying with the global feminist movement today? Would he have allowed his vision to be disrupted and revolutionized by the intervention of feminism? Or, in order to discuss the feminist implications of his legacy, is it even necessary to argue about the positions Malcolm X, the man, might have assumed?

Rather than directly address these questions, I want to parenthetically evoke my own recent experience with one of the persisting themes in Malcolm's political discourse—South African apartheid. When I visited South Africa in September 1991, political consciousness regarding the marginalization and oppression of women appeared to be transforming the character of the battle for democracy there. Not only were women in the various organizations of the Liberation Alliance—the African National Congress (ANC), the South African Communist Party (SACP), Congress of South African Trades Unions (COSATU), and so on—developing creative strategies for involving masses of women in the revolutionary process, they were also challenging the entrenched male dominance in the leadership of their organizations. Although a proposed affirmative action plan for women within the African National Congress was not accepted at the last convention, it was clearly gaining support as a legitimate means of reversing the decades-old assumptions that men deserved the preponderance of leadership positions.

Women in South Africa were also redefining the pervasive political violence (perpetrated by Black organizations such as Buthelezi's Inkatha, but supported by the white government) in terms that included the violence they suffered at the hands of their husbands at home. The women activists whom I encountered spoke of the futility of seeking to eradicate this epidemic public violence while their bodies continued to be battered by the violence defiling their private lives.

Feminist consciousness like this disrupts traditional modes of struggle, and many—men and women alike—in yearning for the simplicity of the "good old days" would wish it away, if such magical solutions were possible. In light of the misogynist attitudes often represented in the media (particularly in film and in the music videos and rap lyrics associated with hip-hop) as the consensus of contemporary young Black men, for whom Malcolm is the ultimate hero, I am led to pose another set of speculative questions that pre-empts the first, since what matters is not the "good old days," or what Malcolm might have become—what matters is what Malcolm's legacy means today. And so, is it the legacy of Malcolm X to wish such a feminist consciousness away? Is it his legacy to long for simple formulations and simple answers? Is it the legacy of Malcolm X to ignore the radical reconceptualization of the struggle for democracy urged by South African women?

Having posed these questions, I want to make a case for the possibility of responding to them in the negative—or, at the very least, for the importance of asking them. I will develop an argument based on the critical connotations of Malcolm's own eventual interrogation of his philosophical adherence to Black nationalism.

MALCOLM'S IDEAS CHANGE

On January 23, 1963, Malcolm X delivered an address sponsored by the African Students Association and the campus NAACP at Michigan State University and later published under the title "Twenty Million Black People in a Political, Economic and Mental Prison." He prefaced his speech with words of thanks to the two sponsoring organizations "for displaying the unity necessary to bring a very controversial issue before the students here on campus. The unity of Africans abroad and the unity of Africans here in this country can bring about practically any kind of achievement or accomplishment that black people want today." On the eve of his assassination two years later, Malcolm seemed to be deeply interrogating the nationalist philosophical grounds that had led him to use racialized metaphors of imprisonment at the core of his analysis of the African-American predicament and to advocate an exclusively Black unity as the strategic basis for emancipatory practice. While the thematic content of his speeches retained previous invocations of Black imprisonment—the dialectics of social and psychological incarceration—what was different about his approach two years later was a more flexible construction of the unity he proposed as a strategy for escape. At what was no doubt a tentative moment in the process of questioning his previous philosophy, a moment never fully developed because of his premature death, Malcolm appeared to be seeking an approach that would allow him to preserve the practice of Black Unity—his organization was called the Organization for Afro-American Unity—while simultaneously moving beyond the geopolitical borders of Africa and the African diaspora.

Because Malcolm was in the process of articulating the pitfalls and limitations of nationalism, I want to suggest that implied in that critical revisiting of his Black nationalist philosophy might be a similar revisiting of the male supremacist ramifications of Black nationalism. This is what he said about Black nationalism:

> I used to define black nationalism as the idea that the black man should control the economy of his community, the politics of his community and so forth. But, when I was in Africa in May, in Ghana, I was speaking with the Algerian ambassador who is extremely militant and is a revolutionary in the true sense of the word. . . . When I told him that my political, social and economic philosophy was black nationalism, he asked me very frankly, well, where did that leave him. Because he was white. He was an African, but he was Algerian, and to all appearances he was a white man. And he said if I define my objective as the victory of black nationalism, where does that leave him? Where does that leave revolutionaries in Morocco, Egypt, Iraq, Mauritania? . . .

While acknowledging the problematic racialization of the North African man whose questioning caused Malcolm to interrogate his own position as a Black nationalist, I would point out that nonetheless, his internationalist recontextualization of the liberation struggle as a "Third World" struggle revealed and accentuated the narrowness and provincial character of the nationalism Malcolm had espoused before that time.

> So I had to do a lot of thinking and reappraising of my definition of black nationalism. Can we sum up the solution to the problems confronting our people as black nationalism? And if you notice, I haven't been using the expression for several months. But I still would be hard pressed to give a specific definition of the over-all philosophy which I think is necessary for the liberation of black people in this country.

These remarks, made in an interview with the *Young Socialist* shortly before his assassination (published in the March–April 1965 issue), indicate that even at a mature stage of the development of his philosophical position, Malcolm did not hesitate to reexamine his ideas and consider the possibility of radical shifts in that position. He was not afraid to explore the likelihood that his ideas could not stand the test of the complexities he encountered in his political travels. During the same international travels, he discovered that in a number of African countries and African liberation movements, women were becoming visible in new and important ways. While I do not wish to appear to ignore the extremely complicated and often contradictory position in which women find themselves within processes of dismantling colonial systems, I do want to suggest that it is appropriate to speculate about a philosophical shift in Malcolm's thinking with respect to the place, position, and empowerment of women—specifically but not exclusively about African women and women in the African diaspora.

POPULAR REPRESENTATIONS OF MALCOLM'S LEGACY

I am not certain about the political path Malcolm himself might have taken if he had not been assassinated at such an apparently critical juncture in the evolution of his political philosophy and practice. My meditations on Malcolm X are not necessarily about the ideas a dead man might have arrived at if his life had been spared; what concerns me more is what I would call the "progressive philosophical space" that can be discovered within the legacy of Malcolm X.

In 1992 Malcolm's legacy is being contested within the realm of popular culture. A number of major battles are currently unfolding, whose aim is to capture this legacy and fix it once and for all. There is the debate around the film on Malcolm directed by Spike Lee. Initially, Spike Lee's argument for replacing the original director, Norman Jewison, with himself, was based on the claim that a white director could never do justice to Malcolm's legacy. Once the film was in progress, Amiri Baraka claimed that Lee himself could not do justice to Malcolm's legacy. What is so striking about the debate is its anchoring point: the very conception of Black nationalism—with its conservative racializing limitations and strong masculinist implications—that Malcolm problematized at the end of his life.

Popular representations of Malcolm's "legacy" abound in contemporary youth culture. As Nick Charles has pointed out, "In death, the X has become ubiquitous, seen mainly on baseball and knit caps. The face, handsome and goateed, peers sternly from T-shirts, jackets and bags. His slogans, 'No Sellout' and 'By Any Means Necessary,' have taken on the dimensions of commandments." This is Malcolm's commodified "legacy," as conjured and evoked in wearable images, flashed in music videos, and sampled in rap songs. Who or what is this commodified Malcolm, the seller of T-shirts and jackets and caps? What does the mark of the X mean to those who mark themselves with this sign that signifies everything and nothing? How is the legacy of Malcolm perceived by those who locate him as a movable image, a wandering voice traveling in and out of music videos and rap tunes such as Public Enemy's "Welcome to the Terrordome" and Paris's "Brutal" and "Break the Grip of Shame"? What does it mean to the youth who catch a glimpse of Malcolm speaking and Malcolm dead, lying in his coffin in Prince Akeem and Chuck D's "Time to Come Correct"? How is Malcolm's legacy constructed in Def Jef's "Black to the Future," in Public Enemy's "Shut 'Em Down"? What is the meaning of the words "By Any Means Necessary," as flashed in bold letters across the screen in the last video?

HUSBAND MALCOLM

Angela Y. Davis's argument centers on the impulse to utilize Malcolm's legacy for the betterment of women as well as men. Yet it is no secret that Malcolm's own relationships with women always seemed to start off on shaky footing. In the end, Malcolm seemed to know how to treat a woman when it was important to him; and no woman was more important to him than wife Betty Shabazz. Here she sheds some light on the subject of just what Malcolm meant to her, as a woman and as a fellow member of his family.

We had known one another for about a year before we married, and up to that time we were "friends," nothing more. He always said that he liked to talk to different sisters, to get their opinion about certain things, and he would always apologize for asking such questions. But he used to ask me questions about my background—personal things—and I just said, when he began his apologies for asking, "Oh yes, brother, I realize that you're just interested in me as a person, as a sister." I remember him saying that there were so many women who, if you opened the door for them or bought them dinner or sent them a card, before you knew it they'd have their wedding dress all ready. He wanted me to know that his interest in me was no more than a brotherly interest. Of course, I knew different.

Occasionally we discussed marriage. He once asked me if I

In assuming a critical attitude vis-à-vis this iconization and, because of its commodified character, this reification of Malcolm's legacy, I do not thereby dismiss my own emotional response of enthusiasm about the sense of closeness the younger generation has for this African-American historical figure. And I do not wish to belittle the sense of pride young people express in Malcolm as an ancestral champion of our rights as African Americans. Young people feel connected to Malcolm in a way I could not have even begun to envision experiencing in my own youth, for example, in a sense of familiarity with Ida B. Wells. (In fact, when I was a teenager, I didn't even know she existed.) From this position of ambivalence, I express my anxiety in the face of the one-dimensional iconization of Malcolm X, because the iconization tends to close out possibilities of exploring other implications of Malcolm's legacy that are not heroic, nationalist, and masculinist.

had ever been married and I said, "No." But once, while teasing him I said, "I lied to you and I want to tell you the truth now: I was married before." I'll never forget the way he looked at me! I quickly told him that I was only kidding and he said to me, "That is something you never kid about." It was obvious that he had a serious regard for marriage.

He had said he didn't want to marry anybody; he wanted to dedicate his life to helping black people. He felt that marriage was a responsibility and he didn't know if he could live up to it. He wondered how he could even begin to tell a female where he would be at every minute of the day. (He was thirty-two years old then and a confirmed bachelor.) After we were married, though, it was the easiest thing to do. He would say, "I'll be here and if anyone wants me he can call me there. . . ."

One of the things he often said was that he didn't spend enough time with the children or with me, but I felt that the time that he did have was spent constructively. Looking back now, I remember that whenever Daddy was home the whole house was happy. It wasn't a time for a lot of big, knockdown, drag-out fights that some people have. Daddy would be home tomorrow and there was always something special cooked, little extra touches added to the house. Measuring it in terms of quality, I think he spent as much time with his family as any other man.

Betty Shabazz, "Malcolm X as a Husband and Father," *Malcolm X: The Man and His Times*, edited by John Henrik Clark. Trenton, NJ: Africa World Press, 1990.

From the vantage point of an African-American feminist, with revolutionary aspirations toward socialism that refuse to go away, I experience myself as, in part, a product of that historical moment informed, in part, by Malcolm's discourse, his oratory, and his organizing. Hearing him speak as an undergraduate at Brandeis University before an audience composed of the almost entirely white student population had a profound effect on my own political development. No one could have convinced me then that Malcolm had not come to Brandeis to give expression to my own inarticulate rage and awaken me to possibilities of militant practice. I therefore feel repelled by the strong resonances of unquestioned and dehistoricized notions of male dominance in this contemporary iconization of Malcolm X. This is not to imply that Malcolm was not as much a perpetrator of masculinist ideas as were others—men and women alike—of his era. What disturbs me today is the propensity to cloak Malcolm's politics with insinuations of intransigent and ahistorical male supremacy that bolster the contemporary equation of nationalism and male dominance as representative of progressive politics in Black popular culture. . . .

IMAGES OF MALE DOMINANCE

A question often posed in connection with the exaltation of Malcolm: "Are you Black enough?" Can this question be posed in relation to Latinos/Latinas or Native Americans or Asians or Pacific Islanders or European Americans or indeed in relation to African-American women who wear the X? Another question: "Are you revolutionary enough?" Are you willing to fight, to die? Can this question be posed in relation to women who wear images of Malcolm?

Thus, my third set of questions: Does the passive reception of Malcolm—adorning one's body with his images and consuming movable video images and voice samples of the hero—fix male supremacy as it appears (and perhaps only appears) to challenge white supremacy? Does the contextualization of bits—infobytes—of Malcolm's body, voice, and political wit amid references to women as bitches, groupies, and hoes invest our historical memory of Malcolm with a kind of vicious putdown of women that contradicts a possible turn toward feminism that some of us might associate with his legacy?

Again, instead of directly addressing the questions, I turn

to Malcolm, the man—and more specifically, Malcolm the husband and father as represented by his wife, Betty Shabazz. In the February 1992 issue of *Essence*, Betty Shabazz reflects on her life with Malcolm—on her love for him and on some of the conflicts in their marriage arising out of the prevailing acceptance of patterns of male dominance in heterosexual partnerships and marriage. "I shared Malcolm," she says,

> but I don't know if he could have shared me to the same extent. He was possessive from the beginning to the end, though I think he learned to control it. . . . All my stress was over the fact that I wanted to work and he wouldn't even entertain the idea. He didn't want anybody to have any influence over me that would in any way compete with his. Each time I left him, that's why I left. . . .

Shabazz says that she left Malcolm three times—after each of their first three children were born.

Like all of us from that generation, Shabazz has been affected by the changing economic roles of women as well as by the rise and circulation of feminist ideas. As she reflects upon her own personal transformation, she does not find it difficult to say: ". . . I think Malcolm probably needed me more than I needed him—to support his life's mission. But I don't think that what I would look for in a man today would be what I looked for in a man then. I was very accepting. I just wanted love. I found a sharing and mature man—and I was lucky."

I want to engage for a moment in some speculative reflection, pausing on the question of whether Malcolm might have sufficiently transformed with respect to his personal relations in order to fulfill the contemporary hopes of his wife Betty Shabazz. My purpose is to try to begin to liberate his legacy from the rigid notions of male dominance that were a part of the ideological climate in which Malcolm grew to personal and political maturity. Considering the willingness of Malcolm to reevaluate his political positions, I would like to think that under new ideological circumstances he might have also reconfigured his relationship with his family—and that if Betty Shabazz were hypothetically to reencounter Malcolm during these contemporary times, she might find more of what she seeks today in the man than the historical Malcolm was capable of providing.

But again I am indulging in speculations about what a

dead man—a man who has been dead for almost three decades—might be like today, if he were not dead, when I have repeatedly insisted that I do not intend to suggest that definitive statements may be made regarding what Malcolm X might or might not have been. So, once more I remind myself that I am really concerned with the continuing influence of both those who see themselves as the political descendants of Malcolm and our historical memory of this man as shaped by social and technological forces that have frozen this memory, transforming it into a backward and imprisoning memory rather than a forward-looking impetus for creative political thinking and organizing. It is highly ironic that Malcolm's admonition regarding the "mental prison" in which Black people were incarcerated can be evoked today with respect to the way his own legacy has been constructed.

RETHINKING REVOLUTION

How, then, *do* we contest the historical memory of Malcolm invoked by Clarence Thomas, who did not hesitate to name Malcolm as one of his role models and heroes? Is it not possible to argue that Anita Hill, in challenging the widespread presumption that male public figures—or any man, for that matter—can continue to harass women sexually with impunity, has situated herself within a complex tradition of resistance? Such a tradition would bring together the historical movements for Black liberation and for women's liberation, drawing, for example, both on Malcolm's legacy and on the legacy of Ida B. Wells, whose antilynching efforts also challenged the sexual violence inflicted on Black women's bodies. This tradition can be claimed and further developed not only by African-American women such as Anita Hill and those women among us who, like myself, identify with feminist political positions, but also by our brothers—as well as by progressive women and men of other cultures and ethnicities.

My interrogation of Malcolm X's contemporary legacy means to encourage discussion of some of the urgent contemporary political issues that some who claim to be Malcolm's descendants are reluctant to recognize. Thus my final set of questions: How do we challenge the police violence inflicted on untold numbers of Black men, such as Rodney King, and at the same time organize against the pervasive sexual violence that continues to be perpetrated by men who claim to be actual or potential revolutionaries? How do we challenge the increasingly intense assault on women's reproductive rights initiated by the Reagan and Bush administrations? How do we bring into our political consciousness feminist concerns—the corporate destruction of the environment, for example—that have been historically constructed as "white people's issues"? How do we halt the growing tendency toward violence perpetrated by African Americans against Asians? How do we reverse established attitudes within the African-American community—and especially in popular youth culture, as nourished by the iconization of Malcolm X—that encourage homophobia, sometimes even to the point of violence, associating such backward positions with the exaltation of the Black man? How do we criticize Magic Johnson's compulsion to distinguish himself as a heterosexual who contracted HIV through heterosexual relations, thereby declaring his own innocence, which effectively condemns gay men with HIV? How can we speak out against racist hate crimes, while simultaneously breaking the silence about antigay hate crimes that occur within the Black community, perpetuated by Black homophobes against Black or Latino/Latina or white gay men and lesbians?

More generally, how do we live and act at this juncture of history—in the five hundredth year since Columbus's invasion of the Americas? What are our responsibilities to the indigenous people of this land where we all now live? To Leonard Peltier, who remains a political prisoner, as Assata Shakur remains in exile? How do we make it forever impossible for sports teams to bear such racist, derogatory names as the Washington "Redskins" and the Atlanta "Braves"?

If in 1992 we talk about the necessary means, as in "Revolution By Any Means Necessary," it might make more sense to figure out the means necessary to rethink and reshape the contours of our political activism. I have a fantasy; I sometimes daydream about masses of Black men in front of the Supreme Court chanting "End sexual harassment by any means necessary," "Protect women's reproductive rights, by any means necessary." And we women are there too, saying "Right on!"

Appendix of Documents

Document 1: Fateful Prediction

The dramatic introduction of The Autobiography of Malcolm X *is a point of interest for the scholar examining the last days of Malcolm's life. Apparently, in many passages of the book, including the very beginning, Malcolm seems to predict the nature of his own death. Malcolm believed himself a marked man based on evidence of conspiracy against him in the last two to three years of his life. However, it seems his predictions of his own brutal death came not just from the politics of his life but from an analysis of what he perceived as a sort of curse of violence upon his family, the Little family.*

When my mother was pregnant with me, she told me later, a party of hooded Ku Klux Klan riders galloped up to our home in Omaha, Nebraska, one night. Surrounding the house, brandishing their shotguns and rifles, they shouted for my father to come out. My mother went to the front door and opened it. Standing where they could see her pregnant condition, she told them that she was alone with her three small children, and that my father was away, preaching, in Milwaukee. The Klansmen shouted threats and warnings at her that we had better get out of town because "the good Christian white people" were not going to stand for my father's "spreading trouble" among the "good" Negroes of Omaha with the "back to Africa" preachings of Marcus Garvey. . . .

Still shouting threats, the Klansmen finally spurred their horses and galloped around the house, shattering every window pane with their gun butts. Then they rode off into the night, their torches flaring, as suddenly as they had come.

My father was enraged when he returned. He decided to wait until I was born—which would be soon—and then the family would move. . . . He believed, as did Marcus Garvey, that freedom, independence and self-respect could never be achieved by the Negro in America, and that therefore the Negro should leave America to the white man and return to his African land of origin. Among the reasons my father had decided to risk and dedicate his life to help disseminate this philosophy among his people was that he had seen four of his six brothers die by violence, three of them killed by white men, including one by lynching. What my father could not know then was that of the remaining three, including himself, only one, my Uncle Jim, would die in bed, of natural causes. Northern white police were later to shoot my Uncle Oscar. And my father was finally himself to die by the white man's hands.

It has always been my belief that I, too, will die by violence. I have done all that I can to be prepared.

Malcolm X and Alex Haley, *The Autobiography of Malcolm X*. New York: Ballantine Books, 1964, pp. 3–4.

DOCUMENT 2: RACE MIXING IN LANSING

The life of the Black Muslim preacher Malcolm X was, according to his own autobiography, filled with symbols and indicators that put him on the path to spiritual and political leadership. In the autobiography, Malcolm speaks often of the time he spent in Lansing, Michigan, in the late 1930s as a black boy who looked and could often act white. This time served as one of many turning points for him, providing him with life lessons about racial discrimination. In the following passage, Malcolm speaks of the "race-mixing" that went on in Lansing and how it affected his perceptions of racial issues later in his adult life.

I used to spend a lot of time thinking about a peculiar thing. Many of these Mason white boys, like the ones at the Lansing school—especially if they knew me well, and if we hung out a lot together—would get me off in a corner somewhere and push me to proposition certain white girls, sometimes their own sisters. They would tell me that they'd already had the girls themselves—including their sisters—or that they were trying to and couldn't. Later on, I came to understand what was going on: If they could get the girls into the position of having broken the terrible taboo by slipping off with me somewhere, they would have that hammer over the girls' heads, to make them give in to them. . . .

From what I heard and saw on the Saturday nights I spent hanging around in the Negro district I knew that race-mixing went on in Lansing. But strangely enough, this didn't have any kind of effect on me. Every Negro in Lansing, I guess, knew how white men would drive along certain streets in the black neighborhoods and pick up Negro streetwalkers who patrolled the area. And, on the other hand, there was a bridge that separated the Negro and Polish neighborhoods, where white women would drive or walk across and pick up Negro men, who would hang around in certain places close to the bridge, waiting for them. Lansing's white women, even in those days, were famous for chasing Negro men. I didn't yet appreciate how most whites accord to the Negro this reputation for prodigious sexual prowess. There in Lansing, I never heard of any trouble about this mixing, from either side. I imagine that everyone simply took it for granted, as I did.

Anyway, from my experience as a little boy at the Lansing school,

I had become fairly adept at avoiding the white-girl issue—at least for a couple of years yet.

Then, in the second semester of the seventh grade, I was elected class president. It surprised me even more than other people. But I can see now why the class might have done it. My grades were among the highest in the school. I was unique in my class, like a pink poodle. And I was proud; I'm not going to say I wasn't. In fact, by then, I didn't really have much feeling about being a Negro, because I was trying so hard, in every way I could, to be white. Which is why I am spending much of my life today telling the American black man that he's wasting his time straining to "integrate." I know from personal experience. I tried hard enough.

Malcolm X and Alex Haley, *The Autobiography of Malcolm X*. New York: Ballantine Books, 1964, pp. 36–38.

DOCUMENT 5: A STEP TOWARD ALLAH

Malcolm spent time in prison after being arrested for burglary crimes. The first two years, from 1946 to 1948, he spent educating himself in his cell, reading books and gaining knowledge on a variety of subjects. Then, in 1948, he learned of the Nation of Islam. At first the Nation was just a way to get out of jail a bit quicker. But the letters his siblings sent him about the Nation's beliefs were the beginnings of a new faith for Malcolm.

One day in 1948, after I had been transferred to Concord Prison, my brother Philbert, who was forever joining something, wrote me this time that he had discovered the "natural religion for the black man." He belonged now, he said, to something called "the Nation of Islam." He said I should "pray to Allah for deliverance." I wrote Philbert a letter which, although in improved English, was worse than my earlier reply to his news that I was being prayed for by his "holiness" church.

When a letter from [brother] Reginald arrived, I never dreamed of associating the two letters. . . Reginald's letter was newsy, and also it contained this instruction: "Malcolm, don't eat any more pork, and don't smoke any cigarettes. I'll show you how to get out of prison."

My automatic response was to think he had come upon some way I could work a hype on the penal authorities. I went to sleep— and woke up—trying to figure what kind of a hype it could be. Something psychological, such as my act with the New York draft board? Could I, after going without pork and smoking no cigarettes for a while, claim some physical trouble that could bring about my release?

"Get out of prison." The words hung in the air around me, I wanted out so badly. . .

Quitting cigarettes wasn't going to be too difficult. I had been conditioned by days in solitary without cigarettes. Whatever this chance was, I wasn't going to fluff it. After I read that letter, I finished the pack I then had open. I haven't smoked another cigarette to this day, since 1948.

It was about three or four days later when pork was served for the noon meal.

I wasn't even thinking about pork when I took my seat at the long table. Sit-grab-gobble-stand-file out; that was the Emily Post in prison eating. When the meat platter was passed to me, I didn't even know what the meat was; usually, you couldn't tell, anyway—but it was suddenly as though *don't eat any more pork* flashed on a screen before me.

I hesitated, with the platter in mid-air; then I passed it along to the inmate waiting next to me. He began serving himself; abruptly, he stopped. I remember him turning, looking surprised at me.

I said to him, "I don't eat pork."

The platter then kept on down the table.

It was the funniest thing, the reaction, and the way that it spread. In prison, where so little breaks the monotonous routine, the smallest thing causes a commotion of talk. It was being mentioned all over the cell block by night that Satan didn't eat pork.

It made me very proud, in some odd way. One of the universal images of the Negro, in prison and out, was that he couldn't do without pork. It made me feel good to see that my not eating it had especially started the white convicts.

Later I would learn, when I had read and studied Islam a good deal, that, unconsciously, my first pre-Islamic submission had been manifested. I had experienced, for the first time, the Muslim teaching, "If you will take one step toward Allah—Allah will take two steps toward you."

Malcolm X and Alex Haley, *The Autobiography of Malcolm X.* New York: Ballantine Books, 1964, pp. 179–81.

DOCUMENT 4: VIEWS OF THE NATION

Malcolm X was a minister in the religious and political organization called the Nation of Islam. His chief duties as a member of this organization were to rally together as many of the black people in America as possible, in order to get them to listen to the philosophies of the Nation. The hope was that if the black people of the United States would listen and respond to the Nation's teachings, a change for the better would ripple through society. The following is an excerpt of a speech Malcolm made at the Harvard Law School on March 24, 1961, in the prime of his life as a Nation minister. It describes the philosophies of the Nation in detail and its lofty goals in terms of change for African Americans.

We thank you for inviting us here to the Harvard Law School Forum this evening to present our views on this timely topic: *The American Negro: Problems and Solutions.* However, to understand our views, the views of the Muslims, you must first realize that we are a religious group, and you must also know something about our religion, the religion of Islam. The creator of the universe, whom many of you call God or Jehovah, is known to the Muslims by the name Allah. The Muslims believe there is but one God, and that all the prophets came from this one God. We believe also that all prophets taught the same religion, and that they themselves called that religion Islam, an Arabic word that means complete submission and obedience to the will of Allah. One who practices divine obedience is called a Muslim (commonly known, spelled, and referred to here in the West as Moslem). There are over seven hundred twenty-five million Muslims on this Earth, predominantly in Africa and Asia, the nonwhite world. We here in America are under the divine leadership of the Honorable Elijah Muhammad, and we are an integral part of the vast world of Islam that stretches from the China seas to the sunny shores of West Africa. A unique situation faces the twenty million ex-slaves here in America because of our unique condition. Our acceptance of Islam and conversion to the religion affects us also in a unique way, different from the way in which it affects all other Muslim converts elsewhere on this earth.

Mr. Elijah Muhammad is our divine leader and teacher here in America. Mr. Muhammad believes in and obeys God one hundred percent, and he is even now teaching and working among our people to fulfill God's divine purpose. I am here at this forum tonight to represent Mr. Elijah Muhammad, the spiritual head of the fastest-growing group of Muslims in the Western Hemisphere. We who follow Mr. Muhammad know that he has been divinely taught and sent to us by God Himself. We believe that the miserable plight of the twenty million black people in America is the fulfillment of divine prophecy. We believe that the serious race problem that [the Negro's] presence here poses for America is also the fulfillment of divine prophecy. We also believe that the presence today in America of the Honorable Elijah Muhammad, his teachings among the twenty million so-called Negroes, and his naked warning to America concerning her treatment of these twenty million ex-slaves is also the fulfillment of divine prophecy. Therefore, when Mr. Muhammad declares that the only solution to America's serious race problem is complete separation of the two races, he is reiterating what was already predicted for this time by all the Biblical prophets. Because Mr. Muhammad takes this uncompromising stand, those of you who don't understand Biblical prophecy wrongly label him a racist and hate-teacher and accuse him of being anti-white and teaching black supremacy. But this evening since we are all here at the Harvard Law School Forum; together, both races face to face, we can question and examine for ourselves the wisdom or folly of what Mr. Muhammad is teaching.

Many of you who classify yourselves as white express surprise and shock at the truth that Mr. Muhammad is teaching your twenty million ex-slaves here in America, but you should be neither surprised nor shocked. As students, teachers, professors, and scientists, you should be well aware that we are living in a world where great changes are taking place. New ideas are replacing the old ones. Old governments are collapsing, and new nations are being born. The entire old system which held the old world together has lost its effectiveness, and now that old world is going out. A new system or a new world must replace the old world. Just as the old ideas must be removed to make way for the new, God has declared to Mr. Muhammad that the evil features of this wicked old world.

Archie Epps, ed., *The Speeches of Malcolm X at Harvard.* New York: William Morrow & Company, Inc., 1969, pp. 115–17.

DOCUMENT 5: ONE OF THE VICTIMS OF DEMOCRACY

Malcolm returned to Harvard on more than one occasion to speak on the problems of the African American living in the United States. During his time in the Nation he made many dramatic speeches that encompassed not just the problems of his people, but also of the American political system in general. Malcolm settled for no less than the complete overhauling of the American system, as demonstrated in the following return presentation of Malcolm X, this time at Harvard's Leverett House Forum in March 1964.

I am not a politician. I'm not even a student of politics. I'm not a Democrat. I'm not a Republican. I don't even consider myself an American. If I could consider myself an American, we wouldn't even have any problem. It would be solved. Many of you get indignant when you hear a black man stand up and say, "No, I'm not an American." I see whites who have the audacity, I should say the nerve, to think that a black man is radical and extremist, subversive and seditious if he says, "No, I'm not an American." But at the same time, these same whites have to admit that this man has a problem.

I don't come here tonight to speak to you as a Democrat or a Republican or an American or anything that *you* want me to be. I'm speaking as what I am: one of twenty-two million black people in this country who are victims of your democratic system. They're the victims of the Democratic politicians, the victims of the Republican politicians. They're actually the victims of what you call democracy. So I stand here tonight speaking as a victim of what you call democracy. And you can understand what I'm saying if you realize it's being said through the mouth of a victim; the mouth of one of the oppressed, not through the mouth and eyes of the oppressor. But if you think we're sitting in the same chair or standing on the same platform, then you won't understand what I'm talking about. You'd expect me to stand up here and say what you would say if you were standing up here. And I'd have to be out of my mind.

Whenever one is viewing this political system through the eyes of a victim, he sees something different. But today these twenty-two million black people who are the victims of American democracy, whether you realize it or not, are viewing your democracy with new eyes. Yesterday our people used to look upon the American system as an American dream. But the black people today are beginning to realize that it is an American nightmare. What is a dream to you is a nightmare to us. What is hope to you has long since become hopeless to our people. And as this attitude develops, not so much on Sugar Hill [in Harlem]—although it's there too—but in the ghetto, in the alley where the masses of our people live . . . there you have a new situation on your hands. There's a new political consciousness developing among our people in this country. In the past, we weren't conscious of the political maneuvering that goes on in this country, which exploits our people politically. We knew something was wrong, but we weren't conscious of what it was. Today there's a tendency on the part of this new generation of black people (who have been born and are growing up in this country) to look at the thing not as they wish it were, but as it actually is. And their ability to look at the situation as it is, is what is primarily responsible for the ever-increasing sense of frustration and hopelessness that exists in the so-called Negro community today.

Archie Epps, ed., *The Speeches of Malcolm X at Harvard.* New York: William Morrow & Company, Inc., 1969, pp. 134–35.

DOCUMENT 6: BY ANY MEANS NECESSARY

In his prime as a preacher of the Black Muslim faith, Malcolm had developed and was spreading one of his most famous of philosophies, "by any means necessary." For Malcolm this meant that the black man had sacrificed enough to the white people of the United States, that he was entitled to use any means to accomplish separation and freedom from white America. This would become a kind of credo for Malcolm in the early '60s. In the following excerpt from a speech, Malcolm explains this slogan at an Oxford University seminar in 1964.

A Black man is supposed to have no feelings. [*Applause*] So when a Black man strikes back, he's an extremist. He's supposed to sit passively and have no feelings, be nonviolent, and love his enemy. No matter what kind of attack, be it verbal or otherwise, he's supposed to take it. But if he stands up and in any way tries to defend himself, [*Malcolm laughs*] then he's an extremist. [*Laughter and applause*] . . .

My reason for believing in extremism—intelligently directed extremism, extremism in defense of liberty, extremism in quest of justice—is because I firmly believe in my heart that the day that the Black man takes an uncompromising step and realizes that he's within his rights, when his own freedom is being jeopardized, to use any means necessary to bring about his freedom or put a halt to that injustice, I don't think he'll be by himself.

I live in America, where there are only 22 million Blacks against probably 160 million whites. One of the reasons that I'm in no way reluctant or hesitant to do whatever is necessary to see that Black people do something to protect themselves [is that] I honestly believe that the day that they do, many whites will have more respect for them. And there will be more whites on their side than are now on their side with this little wishy-washy "love-thy-enemy" approach that they've been using up to now.

And if I'm wrong, then you are racialists.

Steve Clark, ed., *Malcolm X Talks to Young People.* New York: Pathfinder Press, 1991, pp. 20–21.

DOCUMENT 7: THE PROSPECT OF BROTHERHOOD

The philosophies of Malcolm X continued to evolve as he spent more time with the Black Muslim movement. In the beginning, complete separation from the white people of America seemed the only viable solution in Malcolm's opinion. However, over time his view became one of brotherhood of all races. He still believed there was much work to be done before any reasonable connection between whites and blacks could be made in the United States. However, after becoming involved in the leadership of the Organization of Afro-American Unity, and in the final days before his total break with the Nation of Islam, Malcolm became increasingly open (if not necessarily optimistic) of the possibility of racial union in America. The following December 1964 speech, the last of his series at Harvard, reflects this change in attitude.

I'm a Muslim. Now if something is wrong with being Muslim, we can argue, we can "get with it." I'm a Muslim, which means that I believe in the religion of Islam. I believe in Allah, the same God that many of you would probably believe in if you knew more about Him. I believe in all of the prophets: Abraham, Moses, Jesus, Muhammad. Most of you are Jewish, and you believe in Moses; you might not pick Jesus. Well, I'm Muslim, and I believe in Moses, Jesus, and Muhammad. I believe in all of them. So I think I'm "way up on you."

In Islam we practice prayer, chastity, fasting. These should be practiced in all religions. The Muslim religion also requires one to make the pilgrimage to the Holy City of Mecca. I was fortunate enough to make it in April, and I went back again in September. Insofar as being a Muslim is concerned, I have done what one is supposed to do to be a Muslim.

Despite being a Muslim, I can't overlook the fact that I'm an Afro-American in a country which practices racism against black people. There is no religion under the sun that would make me forget the suffering that Negro people have undergone in this country. Negroes have suffered for no reason other than that their skins happen to be black. So whether I'm Muslim, Christian, Buddhist, Hindu, atheist or agnostic, I would still be in the front lines with Negro people fighting against the racism, segregation, and discrimination practiced in this country at all levels in the North, South, East, and West.

I believe in the brotherhood of all men, but I don't believe in wasting brotherhood on anyone who doesn't want to practice it with me. Brotherhood is a two-way street. I don't think brotherhood should be practiced with a man just because his skin is white. Brotherhood should hinge upon the deeds and attitudes of the man.

Archie Epps, ed., *The Speeches of Malcolm X at Harvard.* New York: William Morrow & Company, Inc., 1969, pp. 163–64.

DOCUMENT 8: GLOBAL OPPRESSION

In understanding Malcolm's attitudes about race and racism, it is important to understand that his ideas for social revolution were not just for America but for Africa and the rest of the world as well. Nothing short of global change would satisfy him. The following speech at the London School of Economics in early February 1965, entitled "The oppressed masses of the world cry out for action against the common oppressors," shows an example of this global interest, manifested here in his discussion of "the recent situation in the Congo."

In America the Black community in which we live is not owned by us. The landlord is white. The merchant is white. In fact, the entire economy of the Black community in the States is controlled by someone who doesn't even live there. The property that we live in is owned by someone else. The store that we trade with is operated by someone else. And these are the people who suck the economic blood of our community.

And when you see the Blacks react, since the people who do this aren't there, they react against their property. The property is the only thing that's there. And they destroy it. And you get the impression over here that because they are destroying the property where they live, that they are destroying their own property. No. They can't get to the man, so they get at what he owns.

This doesn't say it's intelligent. But whoever heard of a sociological explosion that was done intelligently and politely? And this is what you're trying to make the Black man do. You're trying to drive him into a ghetto and make him the victim of every kind of unjust condition imaginable. Then when he explodes, you want him to explode politely! You want him to explode according to somebody's ground rules. Why, you're dealing with the wrong man, and you're dealing with him at the wrong time in the wrong way.

Another example of how this imagery is mastered, at the international level, is the recent situation in the Congo. Here we have an example of planes dropping bombs on defenseless African villages.

When a bomb is dropped on an African village, there's no way of defending the people from the bomb. The bomb doesn't make a distinction between men and women. That bomb is dropped on men, women, children, and babies. Now it has not been in any way a disguised fact that planes have been dropping bombs on Congolese villages all during the entire summer. There is no outcry. There is no concern. There is no sympathy. There is no urge on the part of even the so-called progressive element to try and bring a halt to this mass murder. Why?

Because all the press had to do was use that shrewd propaganda word that these villages were in "rebel-held" territory. "Rebel-held," what does that mean? That's an enemy, so anything that they do to those people is all right. You cease to think of the women and the children and the babies in the so-called rebel-held territory as human beings. So that anything that is done to them is done with justification. And the progressives, the liberals don't even make any outcry. They sit twiddling their thumbs, as if they were captivated by this press imagery that has been mastered here in the West also.

They refer to the pilots that are dropping the bombs on these babies as "American-trained, anti-Castro Cuban pilots." As long as they are American-trained, this is supposed to put the stamp of approval on it, because America is your ally. As long as they are anti-Castro Cubans, since Castro is supposed to be a monster and these pilots are against Castro, anybody else they are against is also all right. So the American planes with American bombs being piloted by American-trained pilots, dropping American bombs on Black people, Black babies, Black children, destroying them completely— which is nothing but mass murder—goes absolutely unnoticed.

Steve Clark, ed., *February 1965: The Final Speeches.* New York: Pathfinder Press, 1992, pp. 48–49.

DOCUMENT 9: FRAUD OF THE BLACK MUSLIMS

Eventually, Malcolm broke ranks and left the Nation of Islam. The news of his departure was a shock to the American public, to the Black Muslim movement, and to Elijah Muhammad, arguably the only man higher up in the chain of command then Malcolm himself. On February 18, 1965, just three days before Malcolm's death, a New York City radio personality named Stan Bernard brought Malcolm on to discuss the problems he saw in the Nation of Islam's approach to being a Muslim and his motivations for leaving the official Black Muslim movement in the United States. With Malcolm was friend Aubrey Barnette, who left the Nation with Malcolm and who was one of many to participate in Malcolm's new Muslim Mosque, Inc.

STAN BERNARD: And what is the [Black Muslim] movement? Is it a bona fide religion or just a terror organization? Tonight on Stan Bernard "Contact" we're going to have a look at the Muslims and the Black nationalists in general. And my guest tonight: Malcolm X, once the number-two man in the Black Muslims, now broken with Elijah Muhammad; he says he's a marked man and that a number of attempts have been made on his life. And also in the studio, or we hope very shortly, Aubrey Barnette. . . . He's also split from the organization, and he's written an article in this week's *Saturday Evening Post* labeled simply "The Black Muslims Are a Fraud. . . ." Aubrey Barnette, in your article you call the Black Muslims a fraud. Now does this just apply to the [Nation's] methods of raising money or what? Do you think it's a religious fraud as well?

AUBREY BARNETTE: I think the entire Black Muslim movement is a fraud. And Webster's Dictionary defines a fraud as deceit, trickery, or a trick. The Black Muslims have deceived the public. They've used trickery on trying to attract the Negroes and they have outright tricked the poor Black Muslim members. That's why I say they are a fraud.

BERNARD: Now, okay, they've tricked them. Now this is in terms of the religion itself as well as the money raising?

BARNETTE: Well, as far as the religion of Islam is concerned, I might say right here that any similarity between the Black Muslims and the true religion of Islam is purely coincidental.

BERNARD: Malcolm X, I said at the outset that you were once the number-two man. I think I can rightfully say that, easily you were certainly as well known as, almost as well known, or as well known as Elijah Muhammad.

MALCOLM X: But I never was the number-two man.

BERNARD: You never were the number-two man.

MALCOLM X: The press said I was the number-two man, but there were others ahead of me.

BERNARD: How do you feel about this comment from Aubrey Barnette?

MALCOLM X: What he's saying is true, especially about the first, especially about the religion. The religion of Islam itself is a religion that is based upon brotherhood and a religion in which the persons who believe in it in no way judge a man by the color of his skin. The yardstick of measurement in Islam is one's deeds, one's conscious behavior. And the yardstick of measurement that was used by Elijah Muhammad was based upon the color of the skin.

BERNARD: Malcolm, it wasn't too long ago that you were preaching separation, Black supremacy, you were—or separation at any rate; if not Black supremacy, it sounded like Black supremacy to a lot of people. How do you equate that now with what you're saying today?

MALCOLM X: There's not one person who is a Muslim who believes in Elijah Muhammad today . . . more strongly than I did. When I was with him I believed in him 100 percent. And it was my strong belief in him that made me go along with everything he taught. And I think if you check back on my representation of him while I was with him, I represented him 100 percent.

BERNARD: What is your status now, Malcolm?

MALCOLM X: How do you mean?

BERNARD: Right now. Have you broken—

MALCOLM X: I'm a Muslim. When I—You must understand that the Black Muslim movement, although it claimed to be a religious movement, based upon Islam, it was never acceptable to the orthodox Muslim world. Although at the same time it attracted the most militant, the most dissatisfied of the Black community into it. And by them getting into it and the movement itself not having a real action program, it comprised a number of persons who were extremely young and militant but who could not—and who were activists by nature but who couldn't participate in things. So the inactivity of the movement caused a great deal of dissatisfaction until finally dissension broke in and division, and those of us who left regrouped into a Muslim movement based upon orthodox Islam.

Steve Clark, ed., *February 1965: The Final Speeches.* New York: Pathfinder Press, 1992, pp. 184–86.

Document 10: The Black Muslims Are Afraid of Me

When Malcolm was in New York on February 18, he sat down for one of the last interviews of his life. This time the subject was not the decay of the Black Muslim movement, but instead an attack against Elijah Muhammad as the supposed perpetrator of a conspiracy against Malcolm. The interview, with reporter Timothy Lee, was printed in the New York Post *under the title "Malcolm X and His Enemies" two days after Malcolm's death. In it Malcolm explains his suspicions that he was a marked man about to be assassinated.*

"There is a conspiracy to kill me because the racists know that I now believe the only way to help the Black man in this country is unity among Black people and white people," Malcolm said a scant few days before he was murdered. "Since 1961 there has been a working agreement between Elijah Muhammad and his Black Muslims and the Klan and the White Citizens' Council. They are all interested in keeping the Black man segregated."

Malcolm . . . was talking in the headquarters of the Muslim Mosque, Inc., located in Suite 128 of the Hotel Theresa at Seventh Ave. and 125th St. He had opened the mosque last year when he defected from the Black Muslims.

During his ten years as a Black Muslim he was certainly the sect's best strategist and organizer. In the year after he left, he said, more than 50 percent of the young men quit the movement.

"I haven't even bothered trying to recruit those men," Malcolm said. "That's one of the reasons Elijah's people want to murder me. They're afraid the same organizing skills I used to make the Black Muslim movement what it was will be used against them. When I start recruiting, the Black Muslims will feel it."

Another reason his life was in danger, Malcolm said, was that he testified in court last year that he was forced out of the Nation of Islam because "I had told members of my mosque that Elijah Muhammad was living with nine wives and six children by these wives. But I've since found out it was seven wives and ten children." No wonder he lost so many followers who were interested in moral righteousness . . .

"I've never had a bodyguard," Malcolm said. . . . "Your alertness is your best bodyguard. But there is a threat against my life and there is no people in the United States able to carry out that threat better than the Black Muslims. I know. I taught them."

Steve Clark, ed., *February 1965: The Final Speeches.* New York: Pathfinder Press, 1992, pp. 181–83.

Discussion Questions

1. How does Bruce Perry explain the various difficulties that Malcolm had growing up, both as a young child and as a teenager?

2. Malcolm X's childhood was filled with hardship and suffering. According to Perry, Malcolm was a troubled child in an equally troubled family. Based on the evidence presented in this book, do you think Malcolm's troubled childhood was a result of his social status and poverty or were there other root causes?

3. How does Louis A. DeCaro Jr.'s article present Harlem of the 1940s and '50s? What was it about Malcolm's Harlem that made it so appealing to the impoverished African American community at the time, according to DeCaro?

Chapter 2

1. Many prisoners seem to turn to self-education as a possible way to "pass the time" while serving a jail sentence. Does this seem to be the case for Malcolm, according to William Strickland's article?

2. Malcolm X wrote an autobiography that devotes much time to the hardships he faced both before and during prison. Do you think these hardships are ever exaggerated in such a personal account? Would Louis A. DeCaro Jr. feel that Malcolm's life was really so bad, or would he see it in a different light?

3. According to Rodnell P. Collins's article, what were to be the most important contributions in Malcolm's change of faith and his conversion to the Nation of Islam? Was it family, fellow inmates, or something else?

Chapter 3

1. What is the Nation of Islam? What is the importance of Malcolm's role in this organization? How does William H. Banks Jr. present this role?

2. Based on the articles in chapter three, describe the religious and political dimensions of the Nation of Islam.

3. In comparing the FBI report with the article by Louis E. Lomax, which view seems to you the more accurate assessment of the Nation of Islam? What are the biases of each source?

4. What were the motives for Malcolm's departure from the Nation of Islam, as presented in Jim Haskin's article?

CHAPTER 4

1. Bruce Perry discusses the final years of Malcolm X and his ill-fated role as leader of the Muslim Mosque, Inc. Based on Perry's writings, why do you think the Muslim Mosque failed? Was it simply due to the early and unexpected death of Malcolm himself? What do you think would have happened to the organization had he survived? Is there a place for organizations like the Muslim Mosque and the Nation of Islam in today's American society?

2. In comparing the articles by George Breitman and Karl Evanzz, which seems to come the closest to explaining the truth behind Malcolm's death? Why is his death so mysterious? Do you believe a conspiracy was involved, or is this simply an exaggeration of the events?

3. Karl Evanzz suggests that not one or even two but a whole multitude of organizations were working against Malcolm X in his final year. What was Malcolm's relationship with the authorities, the Nation of Islam, and other organizations during his last days?

CHAPTER 5

1. How do Americans today remember Malcolm X? Was he just a religious figure, or was he something more?

2. What are the differences between integration and separation in terms of race relations? Which philosophy did Malcolm X believe in? Which philosophy did Martin Luther King Jr. believe in? Why did each man believe in these philosophies, and what are the pros and cons of each? Is American society today one of integration or separation? Give examples to support your answer.

3. There is a trend in literature on the subject of Malcolm X and the Nation of Islam to minimize the discussion of the women in Malcolm's life. What was Malcolm's relationship to women? According to Angela Y. Davis, did he have an effect on the black woman of his time and beyond? If so, what was this effect?

4. In the history books that have been written in the last ten or twenty years, Malcolm X is remembered not for his days of drugs and hustling but for his contributions to black pride and culture. What specifically was it about Malcolm X that inspires history to remember him only for his greatness and not for his average imperfections?

5. Now that you have read all the articles in this anthology, what lasting image do you feel accurately reflects Malcolm X? How does this impression differ from the way you may have previously thought of Malcolm X?

CHRONOLOGY

1925

Malcolm Little is born on May 19 in University Hospital in Omaha, Nebraska.

1927

Malcolm's brother, Reginald, is born in Milwaukee, Wisconsin.

1931

Malcolm is enrolled in Pleasant Grove Elementary School (kindergarten). Malcolm's father, Earl Little, is run over by a streetcar and killed.

1938

Malcolm is enrolled in West Junior High School in Lansing, Michigan.

1939

Malcolm's mother, Louise Little, is committed to the state mental hospital in Kalamazoo. Malcolm is placed in a juvenile home. He tells a teacher that his goal is to one day become a lawyer; the teacher recommends becoming a carpenter instead, since being a lawyer is not a realistic goal for a "nigger." Later that year, he transfers to Mason High School in Mason, Michigan.

1940

Malcolm is placed in various foster homes. He goes to Roxbury, Massachusetts, to visit his half-sister, Ella Collins, for the first time.

1941

Malcolm moves to Roxbury to live with Ella. He acquires various jobs, including shoe shiner, dishwasher, and soda jerk. He also occasionally works for the New Haven Railroad. He is now regularly hanging out with criminals.

1943

Malcolm moves to Harlem in New York. He becomes a waiter at Small's Paradise. He is drafted by the army, but he fakes mental illness to avoid service. He acquires the street name "Detroit Red" and is increasingly involved in criminal activities.

1944

Malcolm is indicted for larceny. He goes back to Roxbury and is given a three-month suspended sentence and one year of probation.

1945

Malcolm returns to Harlem.

1946

Malcolm is convicted of larceny, breaking and entering, and carrying a weapon. He is sentenced to eight to ten years in prison. He starts to serve the term in Charlestown Prison. There he begins reading as many books as possible and educating himself.

1947

Malcolm is transferred to Concord Reformatory for fifteen months. While imprisoned he is impressed by letters from Elijah Muhammad and becomes interested in the Nation of Islam.

1948

Malcolm is transferred to Norfolk Prison Colony, Massachusetts, where he continues his self-education.

1949

Malcolm completes his conversion to Islam.

1952

Malcolm is released early from prison after six and a half years and travels to Detroit to meet Elijah Muhammad. It is there that he changes his name to Malcolm X to show his affiliation with the Nation of Islam.

1953

The FBI opens a surveillance file on Malcolm, as it has with all other Nation leaders. He moves to Chicago to live with Elijah Muhammad. Elijah assigns Malcolm the position of minister of the Nation of Islam's Temple Number Eleven, located in Boston.

1954

Malcolm becomes the minister of Temple Number Seven in New York.

1955

Malcolm becomes the minister of Temple Number Twelve in Philadelphia. There he hears for the first time rumors of Elijah Muhammad's adultery.

1958

Malcolm marries Betty Sanders, a nurse, in January. Their first child, daughter Attallah, is born in November.

1959

Malcolm travels to the United Arab Republic, Sudan, and Nigeria as a representative of Elijah Muhammad. As an ambassador for the Nation of Islam, he travels to the Middle East and Ghana. A television documentary titled *The Hate That Hate Produced* fully exposes Malcolm and the Nation of Islam to the TV-watching public for the first time.

1960

Malcolm meets with Cuban leader Fidel Castro in the Hotel Theresa in Harlem. His second daughter, Qubilah, is born in December.

1962

Malcolm gains evidence that Elijah Muhammad is an adulterer. Malcolm's third daughter, Ilyasah, is born.

1963

Malcolm watches the 1963 March on Washington critically, unable to understand why black people are excited over a demonstration that appears to him to be "run by whites." Malcolm is later suspended from representing the Nation of Islam under the pretense of having given the wrong message in a controversial speech about the assassination of President Kennedy.

1964

Malcolm begins collaborating on his autobiography with author Alex Haley. He visits boxing champ Muhammad Ali for a week. He also meets Martin Luther King Jr. for the first and only time. Malcolm officially breaks from the Nation of Islam to form the Muslim Mosque, Inc. He adopts the new name Malik El-Shabazz. His fourth daughter, Gamilah, is born in December.

1965

Malcolm's house is firebombed in the early morning of February 14. Suspects include Nation of Islam members. Then, on February 21, right after beginning an address at the Audubon Ballroom, Malcolm is shot several times and pronounced dead on arrival at Vanderbilt Clinic, Columbia Presbyterian Hospital. Soon after, his wife, Betty, gives birth to twin daughters, Malaak and Malikah.

For Further Research

Malcolm X in His Own Words

George Breitman, ed., *Malcolm X Speaks.* New York: Grove Press, 1990.

Steve Clark, ed., *February 1965: The Final Speeches.* New York: Pathfinder Press, 1992.

———, ed., *Malcolm X Talks to Young People.* New York: Pathfinder Press, 1991.

Archie Epps, *The Speeches of Malcolm X at Harvard.* New York: William Morrow, 1968.

Hank Flick and Larry Powell, "Animal Imagery in the Rhetoric of Malcolm X," *Journal of Black Studies,* vol. 18, no. 4, 1988.

"Malcolm X: A Candid Conversation with the Militant Major-Domo of the Black Muslims," *Playboy,* May 1963.

Malcolm X, *Two Speeches by Malcolm X.* New York: Merit, 1969.

Malcolm X and Alex Haley, *The Autobiography of Malcolm X.* New York: Ballantine Books, 1992.

Bruce Perry, *Malcolm X: The Last Speeches.* New York: Pathfinder Press, 1989.

Biographical Information About Malcolm X

Marcus H. Boulware, "Minister Malcolm, Orator Profundo," *Negro History Bulletin,* November 1967.

George Breitman, *Malcolm X: The Man and His Ideas.* New York: Merit, 1969.

Mark Carnes, ed., *Invisible Giants: Fifty Americans Who Shaped the Nation but Missed the History Books.* New York: Oxford University Press, 2002.

John Henrik Clarke, ed., *Malcolm X: The Man and His Times*. New York: Macmillan, 1969.

Albert Cleage and George Breitman, *Myths About Malcolm X: Two Views*. New York: Merit, 1968.

James H. Cone, *Martin & Malcolm & America: A Dream or a Nightmare*. Maryknoll, NY: Orbis Books, 1991.

Louis Corsino, "Malcolm X and the Black Muslim Movement," *Psychohistory Review*, vol. 10, nos. 3–4, 1982.

Brian Glanville, "Malcolm X," *New Statesman*, June 12, 1964.

Yussuf Naim Kly, ed., *The Black Book: The True Political Philosophy of Malcolm X*. Atlanta: Clarity Press, 1986.

Bruce Perry, *Malcolm: The Life of a Man Who Changed Black America*. Barrytown, NY: Station Hill Press, 1991.

———, "Neither White Nor Black," *Ethnic Groups*, vol. 6, no. 4, 1985.

William Stringfellow, *My People Is the Enemy*. New York: Holt, Rinehart, and Winston, 1964.

Oba T'Shaka, *The Political Legacy of Malcolm X*. Chicago: Third World Press, 1983.

Ted Vincent, "The Garveyite Parents of Malcolm X," *Black Scholar*, March/April 1989.

FACTS AND SPECULATION ON THE DEATH OF MALCOLM X

George Breitman, *The Last Year of Malcolm X*. New York: Schocken Books, 1968.

George Breitman, Herman Porter, and Baxter Smith, *The Assassination of Malcolm X*. New York: Merit, 1969.

Fletcher Knebel, "A Visit with the Widow of Malcolm X," *Look*, March 4, 1969.

Louis E. Lomax, *To Kill a Black Man*. Los Angeles: Holloway House, 1968.

Eric Norden, "The Murder of Malcolm X," *Realist*, February 1967.

RESOURCES CONCERNING THE BLACK MUSLIMS IN AMERICA AND THE NATION OF ISLAM

Aubrey Barnette, "The Black Muslims Are a Fraud," *Saturday Evening Post*, February 27, 1965.

Dominic Capeci Jr., *The Harlem Riot of 1943*. Philadelphia: Temple University Press, 1977.

Theodore Draper, *The Rediscovery of Black Nationalism*. New York: Viking Press, 1970.

E.U. Essien-Udom, *Black Nationalism*. Chicago: University of Chicago Press, 1962.

Eric C. Lincoln, *The Black Muslims in America*. Boston: Beacon Press, 1961.

Louis E. Lomax, *The Negro Revolt*. New York: Harper and Row, 1962.

Elijah Muhammad, *Message to the Blackman in America*. Newport News, VA: United Brothers Communications Systems, 1992.

Wallace Deen Muhammad, *As the Light Shineth from the East*. Chicago: WDM, 1980.

Dean E. Robinson, *Black Nationalism in American Politics and Thought*. Cambridge, England: Cambridge University Press, 2001.

Judith Stein, *The World of Marcus Garvey*. Baton Rouge: Louisiana State University Press, 1986.

Theodore G. Vincent, *Black Power and the Garvey Movement*. Berkeley, CA: Ramparts Press, 1975.

Eugene Victor Wolfenstein, *The Victims of Democracy: Malcolm X and the Black Revolution*. Los Angeles: University of California Press, 1981.

WEBSITES

The First Malcolm X Internet Site, www.malcolmx.de. This site, run out of the Universität Kaiserslautern in Germany (but printed in English) claims to be the first Malcolm X website. This is an excellent site for information not just on Malcolm X but also on black history and African American studies.

Malcolm X, http://afroamhistory.about.com. A comprehensive list of links to many of the key Malcolm X sites on the Internet.

Malcolm X: A Research Site, www.brothermalcolm.net. The University of Toledo, in conjunction with Twenty-first Century Books, put together this thorough guide to researching Malcolm X both on and off the web.

The Malcolm X Museum, www.themalcolmxmuseum.org. A still-in-progress compilation of memorabilia related to Malcolm X, including photos, audio, video, documents, and more. The Malcolm X Museum will soon be open in Harlem as a physical structure, but in the meantime the official website is already very useful.

The Official Website of Malcolm X, www.cmgww.com. Run by the estate of Malcolm X, this website is great for basic information on Malcolm, including a biography and some of his more famous quotes. There is also a eulogy and a frequently asked questions page.

The Smoking Gun: The Malcolm X Files, www.thesmoking-gun.com. A website that explores the mysteries and fascinations surrounding Malcolm's death. It includes an extensive list of printed material related specifically to the assassination.

INDEX